AN ADULT ADHD TOOLKIT

How to Not Just Cope With Symptoms, but Find Focus, Calm, and Success in Chaos

Samantha Williams

CONTENTS

Title Page

Copyright

Dedication

Introduction   1

Chapter 1: The Science Behind ADHD: How the Brain Works and Why It Matters   5

Chapter 2: Identifying Your ADHD Symptoms   17

Chapter 3: Turning Symptoms Into Strengths   29

Chapter 4: Strategies for Improved Focus   40

Chapter 5: Managing Emotions and Finding Calm   51

Chapter 6: Navigating Relationships   62

Chapter 7: Career Success With ADHD   74

Chapter 8: Building Habits for Long-Term Success   82

Chapter 9: Self-Care and Wellness   94

Conclusion   104

References   109

Notes   113

INTRODUCTION

When I was a kid, I had a reputation for being edgy and not paying attention in class. When things didn't always go my way, I had no other outlet other than to throw my proverbial toys out of the playpen. Fast-forward to 20 years later, not much had changed.

Things were *still* not going my way. I was deeply frustrated, and could never quite put my finger on why I was always failing. They tried to help me, but my folks could never quite work out what was going on with me. As an adult, I had no alternative but to help myself.

Well, I could do that but with a little help from a few friends. This story, however, is just as much your story as it is mine. That is to say that you are dealing with what is commonly known amongst medical practitioners, particularly psychotherapists, as attention-deficit/hyperactivity disorder (ADHD).

Understanding ADHD and Its

Impact on Daily Life

Perhaps you suspect that you have ADHD, or suspect someone close to you is suffering from a disorder that is not as uncommon as you may have once thought. In fact, just over eight percent of young children, and two percent of adults in the U.S.A., have been diagnosed with ADHD. Once I got wind of these statistics, I could correlate them with my own behavior in the classroom back in the day (*What Is ADHD?*, n.d.).

I could never sit still in the class, and sometimes, I would even distract the other kids. If my parents and teacher were still around, they would be the first to tell you that I could never seem to get my homework done. And if, by some miracle, there were those days when I *did* turn in my homework on time, it was never done correctly. So much for me always wanting to be perfect.

What Is ADHD? A Brief Introduction

Of course, it had a negative impact on my school life, but we had no idea how much until later. In the meantime, ADHD is characterized by the following (*What Is ADHD?*, n.d.):

- a consistent lack of focus

- hyperactivity

- impulsive, thoughtless acts

In extreme cases, if ADHD is not treated, it could develop into a chronic disorder, which could have far-reaching implications for the sufferer. While the school kid struggles to keep his grades at satisfactory levels, the adult ADHD sufferer continues to struggle to keep himself together, often finding it difficult to function satisfactorily in his career or job (*What Is ADHD?*, n.d.).

He is also hypersensitive to criticism. This would explain why he often has trouble managing close relationships with significant others. But while he doesn't like to be criticized, he is often the first one to criticize himself (*What Is ADHD?*, n.d.).

How ADHD Impacts Daily Life

I would be lying to you if I told you that I didn't have a substance abuse problem back then. Yes, it is true that I never did drugs, but I couldn't go a day without a fantasy story to escape into for as much of the day and night as possible, be it a video game, movie/TV show, or a book. My family would get very sick of me playing the same movie on repeat every day for weeks, sometimes months. And while I wasn't obese in the strictest sense of the word, my eating habits were irregular and unsound, to say the least. I couldn't go a full day without sweets. Sometimes I craved them out of sheer boredom and habit, and other times I craved them to help me deal with emotions I couldn't handle. Once I was of age, alcohol became my go-to coping aid, and later, a big problem. At the time, though, it seemed to be one of the easiest ways to deal with my anxiety without imposing on others (Ellis, 2022).

Little did we know at the time. Turning to substances and other forms of escapism ended up having a domino effect on everything else in my life. It turns out that not only does ADHD negatively impact the sufferer's life, it impacts that of others as well. Not being able to meet deadlines at work surely becomes a case of letting the team down. But as my dad would always say to me, back in the day, I let myself down the most. I don't believe he meant it, but when he reminded me of this, it always felt like he was being mean to me.

Looking Inside Your Toolkit

I won't say that I was scared of him, but one thing I never did was take my frustrations out on Dad. I did, however, yell at my mom a lot, particularly when Dad wasn't around to stop me. Sadly, this became a practice for the way I handled my relationships with men I took a liking to. Whether as a victim or abuser, perhaps you can relate to this.

Not to worry, because this is something we are going to attempt to fix. I'll begin by providing you with your very own adult ADHD toolkit. One of the first tools you'll be given will help you to learn how to identify the symptoms of ADHD, whether in yourself or in others.

But should you identify any of these symptoms, don't worry, because you'll also learn how to use these to your advantage–positively speaking, of course–and with no harm being done to yourself or others. You'll be able to do this because you'll learn new strategies to help improve your ability to focus, manage your emotions, and keep calm.

Don't Stop Thinking About Tomorrow

There is much more to look forward to in this book in terms of improving how you relate to others. And if, like me, you'd like to focus more on your career, there's a lot you can look forward to in that area as well. So far, so good, right? Things are looking up for you, whether you need to address your own behavior or that of a loved one.

But as with everything in life that needs to be done to make it better, we need to start at the beginning. In this case, we'll begin by taking a look at how the brain works. Moreover, we'll look at the science behind ADHD, and why it's important to understand and appreciate how the brain works on our behalf.

CHAPTER 1: THE SCIENCE BEHIND ADHD: HOW THE BRAIN WORKS AND WHY IT MATTERS

My husband used to mock me, not because I'm a woman, but because of my inability to effectively carry out what women have always been famous for: multitasking. So, if my husband wasn't mocking me, was he really mocking the proactive concept of multitasking? Could it be because James was a great believer in doing one thing at a time? Mind you, he did well in his job as a civil engineer in New York, the city that apparently never sleeps.

Too much on the brain? Too many things to do in one lifetime? Do these conundrums smack of ADHD? Could be because while there are still literally hundreds of buildings that remain at risk of collapsing, metaphorically speaking, of course, James' constructions continue to tower above all the rest, again, metaphorically speaking.

Years later, after our divorce was settled amicably out of court, I had to wonder: just how did he manage to do it? Just how did he manage to keep himself together while everything seemed to be falling apart around me? I tried to compare and contrast the impeccable evidence of his meticulous attention to detail with my so-called methods of madness.

But quite clearly, there could be no calm in chaos, and I would not have known how James could do it (and why not me, for crying out loud?). After all, at least half the time of our coexistence, I wasn't paying much attention. And of course, back then, we had no idea that I had ADHD. Of course, it was a shock to my system when James broke the news to me over coffee at our favorite downtown coffee shop that things could no longer carry on as they did, and that we had to part ways.

It didn't matter that I loved him dearly. But if I'm honest with myself, I took him for granted, always depending on him to help me out of every fix I got myself into, most of which I could have avoided had I been paying a little more attention.

Biology, Chemistry, Learned Behaviors, and Coping Mechanisms

I am not running myself down with what I've been saying. I am self-reflecting, giving myself an honest appraisal of my past behavior, and what needs to be done to improve my circumstances and the way I deal with them. I will say that the help of a psychiatrist and therapist helped to point me in much healthier directions. For the first time since before I could remember, they helped me achieve moments of clear thought without the constant background chatter, anxiety, and impulsive behavior. The downside to any pharmaceutical treatment for brain chemistry is that it can be damaging to vital organs and systems, expensive, and only temporarily effective until the brain builds a tolerance. Another thing I had to consider was that no two brains have the exact same chemistry, and thus any medication may or may not have the same effects and side effects. Seeking psychiatric aid with the mindset that it could help short term until I could develop healthier habits and processes that would help me for the rest of my life was the key. This gave birth to the toolkit I am sharing with you today. In later chapters of this toolkit, you too will learn how to overcome your suspected ADHD, or that of one (or more) of your young kids.

In this chapter, however, I'm going to introduce you to the coping mechanisms that you can use to help you manage ADHD, whether in yourself or someone close to you. But before we get that far down the road towards making further progress in our lives, we first need to understand why such things have happened to us, and why they continue to happen, as the case may be.

In this chapter, we go right to the beginning, beyond how we feel as human beings, and how we feel about our circumstances and the situations we find ourselves in. Before we can begin to understand and appreciate the emotions that we go through, we need to understand the biology of ADHD. Let me put it another way: this is an opportunity for you to learn about what makes your brain tick.

Your brain, however, runs on a different program than mine. As I said earlier,, no two brains are the same. Do you recall the times when many of us devotedly camped outside our nearest Apple Store? That was a time when we wanted to be amongst the first to snap up the latest upgrade of our favorite smart devices. And many of these devices were programmed with similar, if not the same, software.

Our differences are something that many of us still need to embrace. After all, life would be pretty boring if we were all programmed the same, right?

ADHD Biology

There are differences in the brains that we've been given, particularly for those of us who have already been diagnosed with ADHD. Indeed, scientists have discovered that there are differences in the nerve networks and neurotransmitters of folks with ADHD. But sadly, these differences have negative consequences for those folks who have been diagnosed with a long-term condition of the brain. The chronic brain condition causes what is known as executive dysfunction, which, in turn, impedes ADHD sufferers' ability to manage their emotions, thoughts, and actions (*Attention-Deficit/Hyperactivity Disorder (ADHD)*, 2023).

Furthermore, ADHD makes it difficult for sufferers to (*Attention-Deficit/Hyperactivity Disorder (ADHD)*, 2023):

- manage their behavioral patterns.
- regulate their mood changes.
- concentrate and pay attention.
- sit still, and keep themselves organized.

While diagnosing ADHD and treating learning disabilities in young children, one expert went as far as saying that because of the biological factors associated with ADHD, it is sometimes difficult to diagnose the condition. He then went on to explain that a deficiency in a specific neurotransmitter, norepinephrine, caused the onset of ADHD (Silver, 2022).

It became easier for me to understand why and how a single neurotransmitter could malfunction, after the experienced psychologist explained that each neurotransmitter (in this case, norepinephrine) required a basic building block (and in this case, dopa) to function properly. He explained that impaired neurotransmitter activity occurs in four working regions of the brain, namely the frontal cortex, limbic system, basal ganglia, and reticular activating system (Silver, 2022).

So, if there's a deficiency of norepinephrine within the frontal cortex region, impaired executive functioning and inattention could occur. A deficiency in the limbic system could cause further inattention, as well as restlessness and emotional volatility. Finally–and this is interesting–deficiencies within the reticular activating system could be responsible for impulsivity, or hyperactivity (Silver, 2022).

ADHD Chemistry

In the case of ADHD, biology and chemistry appear to be interchangeable, and are interlinked. Even so, differences in the brain's neurochemistry persist, thus contributing toward the onset of ADHD. Alongside such differences, chemical imbalances occur as well (Wilkins, 2023).

In order to understand and appreciate the significance of such imbalances, let me summarize how the brain needs to function properly. Firstly, it needs to send and receive electrical signals throughout the body. It does so through the use of neurons. These are essentially the brain's nerve cells. But gaps exist between these neurons, and in order to fill these gaps to allow messages to be transmitted, neurotransmitters, acting as the brain's chemical messengers, are required (Wilkins, 2023).

Also note that pathways in the brain are required to transport the essential neurotransmitter, dopamine, from one region to another. Two such pathways are known as the dopamine reward pathway and the mesocortical pathway. The dopamine pathway allows us to enjoy the taste of our food, and provides us with feelings of pleasure and euphoria, while the mesocortical pathway facilitates the following executive functions: cognition, decision-making, and working memory (Wilkins, 2023).

It goes without saying that when these two pathways are disrupted, impairment of cognitive and motivational functioning will occur. The scientific belief is that such a disruption could be due to an excess of dopamine transporters within the brain. This is unfortunately common for people with ADHD. You've probably heard of Adderall before, and the reason why it has become synonymous with ADHD is because it is a stimulant that is highly effective in correcting the imbalance for those of us who have it (Wilkins, 2023). That said, the list of side effects and warnings that come with taking Adderall make it clear it is not an ideal long term solution.

There is also such a thing known as the Default Mode Network (or otherwise abbreviated as the DMN). It has higher activity in those of us with ADHD than it does in others. This can lead to issues with other networks such as the "task performing network" and the "visual attention system." Overactivity of the DMN can lead to difficulties with identifying what to focus on, as well as how much we focus on tasks (Wilkins, 2023).

Learned Behaviors

Because we are all unique, we will have a set behavioral pattern that is unique to ourselves. Some of these behavioral patterns may have been inherited from family influences, while others may be learned. In other words, you may not be satisfied with the way you're behaving, so will seek out ways to improve your behavior. If not, you may even want to change your behavior altogether.

Could you be thinking more about your actions before diving head-on into something that we may not have imagined doing previously? Well, why not, after all, you do have both the mental and physical capacity to turn your life around. But herein lies the challenge. The spirit may be willing, but the flesh may be weak. And yet still, where there is a will, there is always a way. Truth be told, you must want to change. It's all positive, right? After all, this is what brought you to this book.

Speaking from personal experience, I remain convinced that our past behavior, as well as the way we may still behave today, can influence the way we think. As far as ADHD is concerned, we might even think off the cuff and may simply act out of impulse, only to regret our actions later. Particularly if our behavior is bad–it does harm to us, as well as to others–there are always consequences.

And yet still, acting out of impulse may not always be a bad thing. Indeed, you could very well act out of inspiration, and go on to achieve very great things indeed. Finally, one of the challenges that lie ahead for ADHD sufferers is learning to be patient. Not to worry, because while you're on your learning curve, you can also learn to cope.

Coping Mechanisms

Indeed, for every problem or challenge you are faced with, there must surely be a solution, right? Going forward, *part of the solution* lies in adopting coping mechanisms, bearing in mind that you may be impatient for change, and still stressing under the bellwether of the consequences of your impulsive behavior. But in the extreme, ADHD clients are also introduced to no less than four coping strategies by their therapists (Rivero, 2018):

1. An appraisal-focused (adaptive cognitive) strategy.

2. A problem-focused (adaptive behavioral) strategy.

3. An emotion-focused strategy.

4. An occupation-focused strategy.

What is termed avoidance coping has also been added to the mix. This coping mechanism, I am led to believe, helps us to deal with our emotions, while an occupation-focused strategy will help us cope within the workplace or during the completion of our everyday tasks (Rivero, 2018).

While I can be highly strung sometimes, I can relate to these four proposals. Let me explain. I'm not boasting when I say that I'm pretty good at my job, working as a bibliotherapist. But in the past, I was known to let my clients (both the publishers and readers) down when I acted out of impulse.

I would be right in the middle of a rather taxing academic review, and ten minutes later say to myself, "What the heck, I'll just make myself a cup of tea." Before I start broiling the water, I notice the stove is dirty, so I figure I'll just give it a quick wipe down. Then I notice that I'm on my last few pieces of paper towels, so I go to the storage closet to grab a new roll. I keep on noticing one thing after the next that demands my attention, and before I know it, the day is gone. I can't take a shower, because I decided the curtains needed to go through the wash, I can't wash dishes because I started replacing the disposal in the sink, half the food has gone bad because I left it out while I was cleaning the refrigerator, I misplaced my phone again, and I still haven't made that cup of tea. On a good note, all of my DVDs were alphabetized for a day and half of the living room was vacuumed.

Because this seemingly innocent cup of tea took longer to brew than planned (an impulse disguised with good intentions that has its own set of consequences), I returned to my desk, loaded with regret, wondering to myself how the heck I was going to finish my work on time now that I had wasted all those pre-scheduled hours. But thanks to newly refined cognitive abilities, I can bounce back from any setback faced (Rivero, 2018).

On Using Norepinephrine

For me, the use of norepinephrine was a short-term, stop-gap measure introduced by my psychiatrist, also a short-term therapist, introduced to me by my long-term general practitioner, who also happens to have years of medical experience under his belt. Back then, my GP was reluctant about the use of prescribed medication, firmly believing that I could develop a dependency on it.

But in extreme cases of ADHD, norepinephrine needs to be reintroduced. Remember, I said earlier that a norepinephrine deficiency could cause someone to develop ADHD symptoms anyway. Not only is norepinephrine a form of protein, but it is also a hormone. It is a critical component of the human body's brain, helping it to manage what is known as the *fight-or-flight* response, always necessary when it is faced with danger (*Norepinephrine*, 2022).

Bear in mind that the fight-or-flight response doesn't only help us deal with physical threats. It can also help us manage our emotions or a sense of nervousness whenever we anticipate ahead of time that we're going to be mentally challenged. We can thank our prehistoric ancestors for this response, but today, having no carnivorous dinosaurs or saber-toothed tigers to deal with, we've let our guard down, thus allowing ourselves to become vulnerable to impulsive behavior, or what I'd also like to label as flights of fancy (*Norepinephrine*, 2022).

When a patient is required to address a deficiency in this essential survival ingredient, norepinephrine–now utilized as a prescribed medication–is also used to increase and maintain the patient's blood pressure. This can be helpful when the patient is also dealing with short-term mental and physical health issues (*Norepinephrine*, 2022).

Finally, it's worthwhile reminding ourselves what positive effects the use of norepinephrine can have on the body. Indeed, norepinephrine can keep us alert, arouse us, and help us to pay more attention (*Norepinephrine*, 2022).

How Neural Pathways Are Strengthened Over Time

If, for example, you require prescribed medication to treat a mental condition–like ADHD–you will in all probability be told by your therapist or medical practitioner that you shouldn't expect overnight miracle cures. It is the same as far as neurochemicals, manufactured naturally, are concerned. And of course, the brain's neural pathways don't operate at a similar speed to, say, an express Japanese bullet train. Neural pathways are strengthened with repeated use, and atrophy with time as other pathways are utilized instead. That's why it is possible to lose certain cognitive abilities, like math or language skills, over time if you do not practice them frequently. This also means that learned behaviors, such as habits and coping mechanisms, feel more natural and easy than new behaviors.

That said, there is cognitive work to be done by you, assuming, of course, you are dealing with ADHD symptoms. It's also interesting to note how behavioral change, whether voluntary, impulsive, required, or not, occurs.

Picture it this way: You would have to travel backwards and forwards every day in a safe-to-travel yellow school bus, day in and day out, for at least the duration of the prescribed school year before you can say to yourself that you've mastered the behavioral change skill required. So, your neural pathways–in training, in this case–will get stronger with completed repetitive cycles. Also, note that scientists estimate that it could take up to 10,000 repetitions to master a particular skill before the "associated neural pathway" is developed (*The Neuroscience of Behavior Change*, 2017, para. 01).

But given your legendary impatience, are you prepared to wait that long before positive behavioral change sets in? It I easier said than done. Belive me, I know! It helps to keep in mind that no one really starts out where they want to end up at the first step. No skill is mastered at the first try, and healthy habits are formed over time. As the famous Lao Tzu has often been quoted, "A journey of a thousand miles begins with one step."

Understanding ADHD in Adults

It goes without saying that a better understanding of ADHD will surely help you to better manage your symptoms. This, of course, assumes that you won't be in any mental or physical condition to nip your inattention or impulsive behavior in the bud over a relative period of time. It is, as I suggested earlier, and as any empathic, experienced, and qualified therapist will tell you: Don't expect overnight miracle cures.

Having come this far with your close reading, I feel confident that you will–over time–learn how to identify the telltale signs that your lack of focus or impulsivity may be spinning out of control. This is something I'll introduce to you in the next chapter. But before we get that far, let us close this chapter with an overview of the tools you'll require to manage these troublesome symptoms.

Managing the Symptoms of ADHD and Why It's So Important

To reiterate, typical ADHD symptoms amongst adults include the following (*Living With Attention Deficit Hyperactivity Disorder (ADHD)*, n.d.):

- an inability to follow through on instructions given to you at work

- always feeling restless or impatient

- a derring-do but reckless attitude that influences your willingness to take ill-advised risks

- always feeling anxious or stressed

- not being able to enjoy a healthy, working, or comfortable relationship with any one person

If you can relate to any of the above, don't worry, because you can be taught by a qualified therapist to manage. And if such symptoms are mild and rarely experienced, you could even self-teach yourself out of trouble. But note that under extreme circumstances, responsible medical practitioners may have no alternative but to prescribe medication to help their patients calm down before being properly coached (*Living With Attention Deficit Hyperactivity Disorder (ADHD)*, n.d.).

Finally, once they believe that their clients are ready for it, specialist practitioners could choose to use behavioral therapy or psychoeducation to treat them. Their choice will, of course, be influenced by their patients' unique disposition or the severity of their condition (*Living With Attention Deficit Hyperactivity Disorder (ADHD)*, n.d.). But rest assured, that going forward, no shock therapy will be applied. This archaic and cruel practice is a thing of the past, and in most countries, it is, thankfully, illegal.

CHAPTER 2: IDENTIFYING YOUR ADHD SYMPTOMS

Once upon a time, I started my day with a note to myself. It was nothing nearly as effective as the planning I'm going to introduce you to in Chapter 8. It was nowhere close to the bedtime stories I tell myself these days whenever I lay my head down to rest. You see, that was back then, back when in the chaos of my ADHD disorder, I was so muddled, I didn't know where and how to begin my day.

Back then, in my note to myself, I was going to meet a great guy down at our local pub, a guy who was interesting enough, even kind and decent, who was going to love and leave me with delightfully wicked dreams. Anyway, I concluded my self-indulgent, cringe-worthy note-taking initiative with a reminder to myself that I would make a day to start reading James Joyce's *Ulysses* backwards.

To my mind, I imagined myself as weird and eccentric as Ireland's greatest-ever bard, who closely rivaled England's Shakespeare across the English Channel, and even our very own great satirist, Mark Twain. But if you're as gender-conscious as the rest of the world today, you're probably wondering, where the heck are all the women? Oh, they're there, alright, with stream-of-consciousness extraordinaire, Virginia Woolf, topping my literary reading list.

Recognizing the Signs and Understanding the Impact

Back then, it was never easy for me to follow Joyce and Woolf's stream-of-consciousness narratives, particularly when my own mind was in a continuous state of flux. So, because *Ulysses* and *Mrs Dalloway* were essentially prescribed reading for my major in English literature, I buried them at the bottom of my desk drawer, extricating them only days before cramming for our end-of-year English Lit. exams. A fat lot of good that did me, as it turned out. Not to worry, I did pass. But scraping by is hardly ideal for a future career as a writer, right?

Anyway, another thing that was starting to bother me back then was the level of my ignorance; not so much of those who were blatantly and obviously different from me, but more to do with my own state of mind. I made no time to answer the hard questions on why I was hellbent on stuttering my way through campus life as one of the many underachievers who drop out after their first year of studies. I'm led to believe that this is a trend that continues today, and needs to be addressed. I guess I was lucky to go beyond my first year, and, three years later, finish with a degree, majoring in English literature.

I was ignorant of the potential I had as a professional writer, and came dangerously close to losing out altogether on the rewarding career I now enjoy as a specialist in bibliotherapy (self-help books with a focus on mental health). Finally, as harsh as it may sound at this point, you may already be familiar with the sage suggestion that negative people get nowhere in life.

I was negative, by and large, just like you might still be today, but I guess the fact that I remained a dreamer also rescued me from the brink.

Overcoming Negative Self-Talk

Today, I'm one of the most positive motivational speakers in town. My focus remains on empowering myself with knowledge. I believe that this is necessary before I speak to others who may be less fortunate than I was when I started out. I don't lecture them, and I don't talk too much to them either. I leave them with a few ideas, or motivations, to go out there and empower themselves with the knowledge and practical tools they can use to counter the mental distractions that prevent them from achieving their best.

Funny thing though, while I may not be a cognitive behavioral therapy (CBT) specialist supervising her clients on a daily basis, there is one form of CBT I practice on myself. It works like a charm. Yes, there's a whole lot of talking going on, only the thing is, I'm talking to myself. You may be surprised to learn that such an exercise is not a sign of madness.

Boredom and Negativity

It's quite human to talk to yourself every once in a while. But this internal monologue that only you will be privy to is effective in the sense that you're driving and challenging yourself to move away from your usual distractions, and arguing against your symptomatic ADHD habit of negative self-talk. And on days when I'm feeling mentally fatigued, I make a point of reminding myself that positive things happen to positive people. Here's a mantra that my therapist shared with me, and I'd like to share with you:

Positive thoughts.

Positive feelings.

Positive actions.

Positive results.

Because you're unique, you can motivate yourself with your own thoughts and words, just as long as you keep these positive. If mantras don't work for you, that's okay. Something that has made a difference for me is challenging myself to see the silver lining or hidden opportunity whenever I start forming those dark clouds above my head. Persist with daily exercises like these, and you'll also be able to keep yourself from becoming bored with your life, always looking forward to the positive possibilities that lie just around the corner.

Boredom, of course, happens to be yet another symptom of ADHD. It's almost too easy to reach for a distraction when boredom begins to sink in, even if you're mid-task. This is especially true if it has become a habitual response to boredom. For me, it's my phone. I'll be in the middle of something and my mind will begin to get bored, so I give myself the excuse of just taking a quick break. Too often, that break lasts for hours. If I don't have a distraction handy, or I try to force myself to concentrate, I sometimes fall asleep or my thoughts wander. Have you had similar struggles?

It helps me to take a deep breath, stretch my arms or legs, and gently remind myself that now is not the time for distraction. I'll take another deep breath, and refocus. The effectiveness of this didn't happen overnight. It came after a few months of mindful meditation. We will go over that in a later chapter.

There's one more thing I'd like to talk about before I show you how it's possible for you to recognize the triggers that put you on the spot, completely missing the fork in the road, and driving right through the red light, at risk to yourself, as well as others.

Impulsivity

Impulsive behavior is arguably one of the more prominent symptoms of ADHD. And yet, you may not even recognize that you might have an ADHD disorder, particularly if you're one of those timid folks who are not prone to impulsivity. You would rather play things by ear, and will probably spend hours, days, and perhaps even weeks thinking about what you need or feel you should be doing, or would like to do. By the way, this tentative tendency to spend too much time thinking about something, whether it's important or not, is, quite literally, known as overthinking.

If you are an impulsive person, you may still come to regret your actions, just as a perennial overthinker would regret *not* having done something. So, it goes without saying that if impulsivity is part of your mental profile, you need to learn to slow down and slowly consider every next step you'd like to take, or every decision you'd like to make.

Recognizing Your Triggers

Before you're even able to recognize the triggers that could unleash ADHD in you, it's important to understand and appreciate what triggers in general entail. Briefly put, triggers are not related directly to you. They are external factors, or surrounding extenuating circumstances that could lead you to develop ADHD.

In the meantime, ADHD triggers can be influenced by any one or more of the following (*What Can Trigger ADHD in Adults?*, 2023):

- Differences in brain structure: Apart from neurotransmitter imbalances, ADHD sufferers could also have either smaller or larger brain areas than the average mentally healthy individual.

- Genetic disposition: On a personal level, after I was formally diagnosed with ADHD, I was able to recognize that my mom also had typical symptoms of the disorder.

- At-risk people: You could develop ADHD if you were born prematurely (usually before 37 weeks), suffer from epilepsy, or sustained brain damage through a head injury or even while still in your mom's womb.

But if none of the above applies to you, you would have to become aware of the external factors that could bump you up into a low-level category of ADHD. So, take note of environmental factors (a polluted, congested living environment), lifestyle habits (excessive late nights at noisy venues), and work-related or everyday tasks (high-pressure environments which usually include high volumes of work) (*What Can Trigger ADHD in Adults?*, 2023).

Dealing With Frustration Tolerance Levels

No matter how healthy you are mentally and/or physically, you could still be prone to unmanageable frustration tolerance levels, brought about by the external factors that surround you, or your inherited genetic composition. Arguing with my mom that she may have ADHD is not a solution. And at her age, she's so set in her ways, that there's very little I can do to motivate her to change her behavior.

But while praying the Rosary on a daily basis works for her, mindfulness meditation keeps me less frustrated and more tolerant of myself, as well as the circumstances that led to me being excessively frustrated and intolerant in the first place. Indeed, it's a good idea to embrace the mindfulness philosophy because, with time and practice, it can work wonders in terms of letting you cope better emotionally, and help you to better understand the triggers that may have engulfed you (*What Can Trigger ADHD in Adults?*, 2023).

Aggression and Irritability

A prescribed course of anger management may be in the cards for folks who tend to act out a lot more aggressively than others. This is what happens when things don't go their way. They are angry and frustrated, and there is very little that won't irritate them. And if they don't come to blows with others, they can be rude beyond borders. I can remember feeling this way.

If I wasn't ashamed of myself, I would be embarrassed, which made me even more prickly. It was never within my nature to lash out, and moments after the physical or verbal conflict occurred, I would regret what I had done. Because such aggression wasn't typical of me, it would enter into a dormant state, but could re-emerge to rear its ugly head months later. All it would take was a family crisis, or financial jam that I couldn't seem to get myself out of.

But in the meantime, the irritability would continue. Self-help therapy may not be enough to rescue an ADHD sufferer who is characteristically aggressive and always irritated by others. But if she is someone who generally keeps to herself, even when she's about to snap, she could be at risk of doing harm to herself. I for one, am prone to self-sabotage without meaning to. It's almost like a part of my mind knows I'm uncomfortable with feeling like I'm getting away without punishment for my actions, and it seeks to remedy that with more poor, spur-of-the-moment decision making.

Anxiety

By far, the most common symptom of ADHD is anxiety. If you were a concerned parent or friend, however, you wouldn't always know what your child or friend was going through, unless he or she spoke out. By the anxious expression on his or her face, you would certainly know that something is wrong or bothering them, but would not know whether they're suffering as a result of ADHD.

The best way to know would be to have a more acute understanding of ADHD's symptoms. In the meantime, whether it's anxiety, anger, frustration, or just the blues that's bothering you, there are practical things you can do to start helping to reduce those symptoms. You may not be in a position to release the ADHD triggers altogether, but you can at least manage them by:

- following a healthy, balanced diet.

- exercising and keeping yourself physically active as much as possible.

- limiting the amount of time you spend in contact with others online. Limit your online time if your behavior is voyeuristic.

- taking up meditation, and practicing mindfulness (What Can Trigger ADHD in Adults?, 2023).

By all means, plan ahead to make sure that you're able to get through the day, and enjoy a more fulfilling life. This book's final chapter will offer you a few practical guidelines on how you can plan and organize like a pro (*What Can Trigger ADHD in Adults?*, 2023).

That said, a full-blown panic attack, or even a small panic, isn't always easy to recognize. There are the classic symptoms of hyperventilating, or feeling like you're having an out of body experience, but attack symptoms can also be more subtle. For some, it's feeling like you need to get away quickly, or suddenly lashing out for no apparent reason. For me, the most terrifying thing was not knowing what was going on with me. Once I was able to recognize what was happening, I could also recognize where I was in my attack and I would ride it out like a pro surfer rides a wave, making it back to shore safely instead of being pushed and twisted around underwater. Realizing I was having an attack helped make it less severe and terrifying. In time, I was able to not just ride it out, but calm myself down completely using the 5,4,3,2,1 grounding method. This method is simple once you know it, but it might help having someone coach you through it until you are able to do it on your own.

The first step is looking around and listing five things you can see. The next step is listening and saying four things you can hear at that moment. The third step is pointing out three things near you that you can touch. Then, list two things you smell. The last step is naming one thing you taste. The point of the exercise is to not just bring you back to the moment, but calm the mind down. Taking the time to do this can help calm the "fight or flight" sympathetic nervous system down enough to realize there is no real danger in that moment. This system may have helped our ancestors escape predators, but it doesn't do us much good when we are having a talk with a colleague or family member and something in the conversation feels scary.

The Constant Flow of the Mind

One of the best ways for me to calm myself down is to observe the sea's waves, how they meander their way onto the beach, and after seeming to take a deep breath, wondering whether or not to soak into the sand, ooze their way back into the great gulf of the sea. It is a constant flow that never stops, it ebbs and flows, and ebbs and flows, all over again. . . until such time as the weather decides to change.

Today, whether you live near the coastline or not, it doesn't seem to make much of a difference. One way or another, the weather always seems to be bad. Today, there's a lot of talk of this being climate change, and as I sit on my favorite bench down by the waterfront, I often think about the damage we've caused to allow Mother Nature to raise hell in the way she has been doing lately.

And today, while I'm essentially a gentle soul by nature, I still find myself having to use the inclement weather as an apt metaphor to describe the constant flow of my mind's innermost thoughts, usually not being able to make much sense of it either.

How Stream-of-Consciousness Works

I have decided to utilize literary persuasion, rather than a clinical definition, to explain how stream-of-consciousness works. These are also thoughts that I picked up during my varsity days when I was studying languages, literature, and creative writing. I'm providing you with the literary description because I think it will make the understanding and appreciation of stream of consciousness a little easier on the restless soul that can never seem to sit still.

Shall we give this literary definition a try, then?

So, if you allow your stream of consciousness to work with your changing thoughts, after observing others and listening to them, you'll be dialing into their thoughts as well. But you need to use your literary or language skills to closely mirror their thoughts which, like yours, and like the waves rushing into the beach, are continuously changing (*Stream of Consciousness*, n.d.).

A simple, literary definition of stream of consciousness describes it as a style or technique of writing that attempts to capture a natural flow of a literary character's extended thought processes. Stream-of-consciousness does this by grasping sensory impressions and incomplete ideas, as well as making use of unusual syntax and coarse forms of grammar, just like the great James Joyce did in his *Ulysses* (*Stream of Consciousness*, n.d.).

Basically, it mirrors the internal, constantly changing and sometimes interrupted internal dialogue and thoughts we have moment by moment. And to continue the metaphor, if an earthquake begins in our mind and we allow ourselves to follow the waves it makes, we can end up finding ourselves washed away in a destructive tsunami of emotions and knee-jerk reactions.

Understanding Emotions and Moods

Stream-of-consciousness makes use of what is known as associative thought, as well as repetition, both of which could be used for us to better understand stream-of-consciousness as a work in progress. That said, associative thought attempts to merge ideas and loose connections, based on our personal experiences and memories (*Stream of Consciousness*, n.d.).

Repetition, on the other hand, requires little explanation, and perhaps you, too, can relate to the experience. Particularly when you are nervous and your thoughts are in a tizz, how often have you repeated yourself to the receiver of your dialogue? And how often have you noticed how impatient or irritated that person becomes in hearing the same thing, over and over again? You can surely relate to *that* if you are often irritable yourself (*Stream of Consciousness*, n.d.).

It all depends on what mood you're in. Whether it's bad or euphoric, it could last for hours. Heightened emotions, on the other hand, last no more than a few minutes. When comparing moods and emotions, and the impact these make on our mental well-being, we can parse these with triggers. Psychologist and pioneer of micro-emotions, Paul Eckman, believes that it's a lot easier to identify emotional triggers than it is to locate the trigger for our moods (Ekman, 1994).

But by taking into account the five factors that characterize the rivalry between moods and emotions, observing them, and perhaps even studying them, we could perhaps better understand what triggers our moods and emotions–as well as that of others– to the point of distraction. That said, variations in duration, provocation, modulation, facial expressions, and an awareness of causes, also help us to locate the differences between our moods and emotions (Ekman, 1994).

But all good and well that we are now able to connect with our moods and emotions. We're also able to identify the triggers that cause us to be in the moods we often find ourselves to be in, and we're able to dig a little deeper into locating the root causes of the condition we find ourselves in. But more times than not, we're still not able to temper our moods and emotions. Not to worry, because in the next chapter, we're going to learn how to turn our symptomatic weaknesses into our strengths.

CHAPTER 3: TURNING SYMPTOMS INTO STRENGTHS

I don't know about you, but I had a tendency to avoid that which was most important to me. It wasn't necessarily something I was passionate about, or something I dreamt of accomplishing someday–these things were always in the back of my mind anyway–it was things that needed to be done, whether during the day, or before the end of the month. Like getting an important job done before its due date. The job was important because of what it was going to achieve for the client I was working for.

But as far as I was concerned, it was usually more important that I get paid so that I could pay the month-end bills. But if I could truly be honest with myself, it was usually so that I could head off down to my favorite mall, enjoy a latte, and indulge myself in a round of shopping by impulse.

I had a tendency to put all that was really important off. Why was this? Could it be that I was scared that the client might not like what I was going to produce for her? Could it be that I just didn't like the job that I was doing? Was I only doing it for the money? Or could it be that my mind was always flitting from one thing to another, always towards something nowhere remotely close to what I was supposed to do in that present moment? Why was I procrastinating so much?

Could it be that you, too, can relate to what I'm saying? Are you thinking the same things that I was thinking about when

I had no idea of how I was going to extricate myself from the chaotic confusion of my mind, always trying to be in a million different places, all at the same time? Could it be that, like me back then, you're feeling so weak and helpless? Not to worry, because in this chapter we're going to turn your ADHD symptoms into your strengths. That's ideal because it will be helpful to help you counter the problematic, yet realistic, awareness that current thoughts and habits simply cannot be reversed or overturned overnight.

In the meantime, I still believe in miracles, particularly those that have been given the benefit of scientific evidence-based testing. And of course, as I'm sure you'll agree, miracles don't occur overnight.

Harnessing Hyperfocus, Creativity, and Other ADHD Traits

It is one thing to be able to cope with our ADHD symptoms, but it's quite another thing when we continue to stutter and lose focus. The mind is still not calm, and nothing ever seems to get done. The mind continues to operate in hyperdrive, like Han Solo's rickety spacecraft warping into another universe to escape the evil chasing him. The force beckons, but Solo is not yet prepared or ready to embrace it.

Oh, don't you wish you sometimes had the grace of Princess Leia? Don't you wish you had the bravery of a younger version of Luke Skywalker? May your wish be fulfilled in this chapter as we attempt to unravel the mind and turn it into a haven of serenity. And then let us thrive in chaos if chaos chooses not to leave us.

Here, you have clear and present evidence of my mind being at its creative best. If not that, it is trying to be as creative as possible in order to make the most of a challenging state of mind. Through its creativity–with words, in this case–it continues to search for focus and calm, and it believes that it will be successful in chaos, should chaos choose to stay with it. It is also trying to make the most of being hyper-focused.

Hyperfocus just happens to be one of the most common symptoms of ADHD. It is the ability to focus with great intensity on a subject or task of interest, not just for a few moments, but for hours at a time. But let me be honest with you, one aspect of this hyperfocus ability that concerns me is that it might be zoning into something that is not important in relation to the circumstances we're called on to deal with (Flippin, 2023).

How to Embrace Your Strengths and Weaknesses

This may come as a bit of a surprise to some, but I used to be a big fan of playing video games. Some people binge TV shows, some will watch back to back movies. While I do that, too, until the wee hours of the night, I was also guilty of wasting entire days and nights playing games almost all the way to the end, with every side mission done, every character fully leveled up, and every cut scene unlocked. My phone would have missed calls, my to-do lists would be shot, and I would forget to eat or sleep. Mind you, I would often have a cup of tea next to me that was hot at one point during the day, but I would forget I even had it, or that I was thirsty, and I would eventually take a swig of a disappointingly tepid drink. I would be so intent on getting every achievement in the game and playing it through to its entirety that everything else faded away. I did this when reading fiction books, too, to the point that if someone broke my concentration too suddenly, the return to reality would be downright jarring for me. Do you also have something that draws you in so much that you lose yourself for extended periods of time?

Without control, this hyperfocus was very destructive to multiple aspects of my life. I know an alarm wouldn't work, anymore than the clock above the TV ever did. I might see the time, but I'd convince myself that I would just finish this one level, or do this one last quest. Two hours later, and I was still playing. I never thought I would be grateful for wireless controllers running out of battery and needing to recharge. I situated the couch so that it was just far away enough that if I were tempted to continue playing with the controller on a charging cable, it would be an uncomfortable stretch. I also only allow myself to play once a month so that I don't form an addiction to the game, which happens.

It's not all bad, though. Being able to immerse myself so fully in a story came in handy, particularly when I was reading a book for class or studying history. It was like a movie playing in my mind that I was a part of whenever I got into any story. Because it felt like I was there, I could remember characters, plot lines, and mundane details. This immersion really helped, but only if I didn't get knocked out of the zone and distracted by something easier to hyperfocus on.

Based on what you've read so far, you might be tempted to forswear that I am one of the most weak-willed people you've come across. And yet, while you may flinch, you are kind, because what I've said so far about myself might remind you of how weak you may have been yourself. Even so, don't you sometimes wish you could tap into your inner strengths? Your wish can be fulfilled because, over time, you'll come to realize that you have the strength to overcome challenges that will inevitably pop up.

It becomes possible for you to overcome your weaknesses once you've managed to embrace them. This doesn't mean that you're going to throw in the towel, resigning yourself to living with your weaknesses as a weak-willed person. In fact, it is part of what makes you stronger, and if you're one of those who have been overwhelmed by your innate strengths, or have refused to accept that you have it in you to overcome your mental challenges, then now is the time for you to accept and embrace those talents as well.

Allow me to elaborate. I have heard it said by some that tragedy is simply having the wrong skill set for the challenges at hand. Like a wallflower in the world of sales, if we don't recognize our shortcomings, we could end up going down a path that isn't the best fit. However, what would be a weakness in one area, can be a strength in another. To continue the example, introverts are not known for being outgoing networkers, which is almost a necessity in sales. Take that same introvert and put them in a place where they can work on their own, or one-on-one, for extended periods, say as a psychologist or writer, and they could thrive where someone who is more social and outgoing would suffer.

It is now just a matter of harnessing your strengths while learning to overcome your weaknesses, in this case, any one of the ADHD symptoms that you identify with. If you're not able to do this on your own, or are not yet ready to do this, you can seek out the help of those who could help you. Ideally, you will seek help from someone you can trust, whether this is someone at work, or someone you love very much indeed (Kouly, 2023).

Finally, once you've managed to identify your strengths, it's time to work towards developing them. You will, however, need to set aside time to practice. During such practice sessions, you'll be refining what were always your natural abilities. This will allow you to go on to perform better than you ever imagined you could, and as an impulsive person, you'll acquire skills that can help you to restrain yourself whenever you feel the itch to act out of order (Kouly, 2023).

All About Organized Chaos and How to Deal With It

Have you ever heard the expression: there's a method to my

madness? Well, I heard it often enough during one of my many internal monologues I engaged in, in order to reassure myself that everything that I was doing in that moment would turn out okay. Just okay? Why not brilliantly? And yes, you are so right, it was my stream-of-consciousness talking to me as well! So, I didn't need to hear it from anyone else, who may have disapproved of my pretensions anyway. That said, I learned to accept that this was nothing more than an excuse to myself to get out of acting responsibly.

Like you today, I yearned for order to replace the chaos. But as I said earlier, don't expect overnight miracles. It is all good, because you can learn to manage the chaos of your mind by learning to live with the chaos (at least for a while until you're able to overcome it), accept that you'll still make mistakes, leverage them, and train yourself to plan ahead and make better decisions before jumping head first into the fire, metaphorically speaking, of course (Lema, n.d.a.).

Finally, while you're still learning to live with the chaos, you still need to lift yourself up. Listening to others talk you down obviously hasn't helped. Even listening to well-meaning advice from those who care, or say they do, and those who have concerns about your performance, or lack thereof, particularly in the workplace, doesn't always help either. Well-meaning advice, to my mind, is still unqualified advice, and if it's unqualified, it could be blatantly wrong, so much so that you could end up making things worse for yourself. Until you're able to utilize qualified or professional advice, there's no harm in talking to yourself.

When Creativity Piles Up

Speaking from experience, the idea of talking to yourself is not crazy. I still do it today. It works. Let me use a real-life example. Imagine having to do three jobs instead of one. All three projects are invigorating, but you're not doing it for the love of it, you're doing it because you need the money. This is also me talking to myself, by the way, and with the pressure of looming deadlines mounting, and too many distractions to fathom, I was about to crack.

I literally had what my ex-husband dubbed "creativity piles." They were the piles of half finished projects, hobbies, unfinished books, and games that littered our house. A physical manifestation of the chaos in my mind. If my work wasn't going well, I would give myself the excuse of needing a quick break, and I would start cleaning up a pile, only to be sucked into whatever was in the pile. Half a day later, you can only imagine how I must have felt when I snapped back to reality and saw how little time I had left to finish my work.

That was then, and this is now. I have adopted Minimalism, which helps me keep creativity piles in check. It also helps to keep from feeling overwhelmed by how much needs to be cleaned or done, which is usually followed by a period of depressed inaction. We'll talk more about Minimalism and its benefits in a later chapter. Yes, I do still drop what I'm doing, but this time, what I do next is mindful. And one of my favorite mindfulness activities is taking my muse for a walk. It's usually not longer than 10 minutes out, and 10 minutes back, and I've long since mastered the ability to keep my lips still while decluttering and reordering the creativity that was piling up while I was still at my desk, sans physical creativity piles.

By now, the spark in my brain is shining brightly and littered with new ideas. It's not so much something new to write about, but more to do with completing what work I still have to do in a more proactive and disciplined manner. I've also learned to work through shorter sessions, timing myself to perfection before the next break bell rings. The break is short too, and I'm refreshed and eager, but not anxious, to get things done.

Leveraging Hyperfocus

If you're a victim of the ADHD symptom of hyperfocus, also known as intense fixation, you can learn to remaster your thoughts and the actions that may follow. By now, you probably know from past experience that it's not always possible to talk yourself out of your hyperfocus state of mind. What you can do, however, is set up external cues to help redirect where your hyperfocus has been leading you to go or act (Flippin, 2023).

But by now, you're probably wondering: how the heck do I pull off this stunt? You could start by bracing yourself, usually with a deep breath, holding it in for a few seconds before letting it out slowly. Do this simple breathing exercise by repeating what I've just suggested a few more times until you start to feel calm. When your mind is calm, your thoughts become more lucid. It is also more accepting of your circumstances, particularly if they're hellbent on challenging you.

While the work you're doing needs to get done, there's no need to tie yourself up in knots, or run away from the pressure. As I mentioned previously, you can harness yourself mentally by putting yourself through shorter, timed work sessions, and reaping the rewards of more but shorter breaks in between. But what if you're one of the lucky ones? What if the work you do engrosses you, so much that you never want to leave your desk or workbench?

What Draws You In?

You're lucky in the sense that you really enjoy what you're doing. It's not so much the money that attracts you to spending more time on the job. If you're an artist like me, it might be more a case of you deriving aesthetic satisfaction from the work you're doing. You could be someone who enjoys doing good for others. Yes, your work is helping you, but you derive more satisfaction from the work because it is helping others more. And when the job is done and delivered, you enjoy seeing the smile on other people's faces.

Until one day it happens. You were able to zone in for so long, so much so that nothing could tear you away from your post. You could not, or chose not, to notice what was happening to your body and mind, until one day, your body *and* your brain decided: enough is enough. Both body and brain wanted to zone out. And if it couldn't do that, it would simply stop altogether, metaphorically speaking, of course. It's like the entire factory in town closed down. Service delivery came to a halt, and more people than you could care to know suffered as well.

Truth be told, there are consequences for letting your enthusiasm and impulsivity run away from you like this and not taking time for breaks. If this is the case for you, it's probably time for you to take a raincheck on this form of potentially destructive behavior. It's time to draw a deep breath, and after a momentary pause, let that breath all out again.

Putting a Check on Energy Levels

It's good to have creative energy. But it's no good if all that creative juice ends up running down the drain, going nowhere. So, don't waste your creative energy, and don't throw it away either. Rather, learn how to use it better, learn how to look after it, and keep it healthy always. Time to turn down the volume, and surround yourself with peace and quiet. Make sure the chair you're sitting in is comfortable as well (Rysdyk, n.d.).

Don't make the chair *that* comfortable, so much so that you could fall asleep in it. Remember, you're tired from all your previous energy splurges, just the same as you might have been from maxing out on your cards at the mall. While you could have carried on for hours, any happiness or excitement may have only lasted 30 minutes. That's enough to make anyone depressed.

Let's put some of that creativity to use with a visualization exercise. Breathing remains the focus, but this time, close your eyes while you allow your breaths to be quiet but full. It is almost as though you were entering into a deep sleep, so peaceful that you wouldn't want to break the siesta. Now, for every breath that you take, there's a light shining brighter until it fills you up. You are radiant. Your body is now becoming an expression of creative energy (Rysdyk, n.d.).

Take a few moments to reflect on these few shining lights. Grasp them with confidence so that you never need to let it go again. These peaceful moments that you will be enjoying are what help you to focus, and it goes without saying that they'll help to keep you calm as well. The goal of this little meditation is to help you control your creative energy a bit so that it isn't getting the better for you, but isn't dampened, either. We'll go over mediation more in the next chapter.

Creative Genius Unleashed!

But before you get there, try to continue pausing and reflecting where all that creative energy came from. Remember, there's no one-size-fits-all coat hanger of ADHD symptoms that we must all dress ourselves up with in the morning before we realize that we've gone overboard. Our bodies and minds all react differently. Take your time with this–dare I say–creative exercise, and by all means, take notes as you go along. No-one wants to forget, but it is good to want to forgive.

This, then, is a great opportunity for you to be kind to yourself. Finally, once you've collected enough notes on the thoughts you've been having about your most recent energy surges, spend a few moments (or more, because there's no need to rush) thinking where to store that energy, and how best to dispense it from now on. Chapter 7 might be helpful in this regard, because it focuses on achieving career success, in spite of having to put up with ADHD as well.

You've got this. You can do this. All you need to do is focus.

CHAPTER 4: STRATEGIES FOR IMPROVED FOCUS

Halfway through our adult ADHD toolkit, we have barely scratched the surface of what needs to be done to improve your circumstances. There is work to be done, but not to worry, because the work you'll be doing to improve your circumstances will be manageable. You'll get used to these ongoing tasks after a while, and the longer you persevere with them, the more you'll end up enjoying them.

I'm certain of this. I've made improvements in my own life. And seeing how these improvements have benefited me, I'm compelled to impart these to you.

So, in the context of this chapter, what can be done to help improve your focus? What can be done to prevent you from procrastinating? What can be done to help you avoid that which is inevitable, and avoid zig-zagging into a multitudinous flurry of tasks that you've deceptively labeled as tasks brought about through inspiration? It is hardly what came to be known as a Eureka moment, particularly since your circumstances haven't improved much, if at all.

Apart from introducing you to techniques and strategies that help you to prioritize and fulfill important tasks, I'd also like to talk about what is known as the "less is more philosophy."

Tips and Techniques for Staying on Task

It seems contradictory, but you can often achieve more by doing less. Also, the quality of the tasks you will be able to complete will be greatly enhanced.

You can begin this realization by imagining that you are studying for an end-of-year exam.

Before, I used to cram in half a dozen theoretical texts in order to try and make sense of James Joyce's stream-of-consciousness movements, and his deliberate abuse of the English language. But once I learned how to schedule my reading, research, and writing time effectively, I could calmly focus on covering just a few pages at a time, and create my own thoughts of what I read and discovered before transferring them to the page. Initial thoughts were mostly subjective, but these did not deter me because I knew that I could now explore theory in order to provide a more lucid and objective explanation of what I was thinking initially.

This was me back in the day. It was also the sum result of my transformation during my first battle with ADHD. Today, you might have something else in mind that you would like to imagine yourself doing, so, for the time being, feel free to exploit your imagination to your heart's content.

Before learning how to create routines that work for you, I might as well add that, going against the grain of my own personality and emotional reasoning, it's a good idea to switch from thinking with your heart to thinking with your head. Believe me, it's worth the sacrifice, and if you're patient, love will still come knocking on your door, in ways that may surprise you, just as it did for me.

Creating Effective Routines

Once upon a time, I used to think that routines weren't just tedious, but downright meaningless. However, once I saw how the elderly who have no alternative but to go about their tasks at a pace so much slower than ours, could make peace with their daily routines, I decided that it was high time that I introduce routine to my daily life as well. I could see how, contrary to my own failings, these folks could accomplish one task at a time, and everything that they needed to do, from getting to the doctor on time, to putting food on the table, all in a single day. Everything that they tasked themselves to do was done on time, bang on schedule.

I soon discovered that routine never needed to be boring. It was just a matter of making it fun. I also discovered that the following tips helped to make my new routines effective (McRae, 2019):

- Set small goals by breaking each large goal into smaller, achievable goals.

- Prepare a plan ahead of time to help you achieve these smaller, incremental goals.

- Prepare yourself mentally for the routine, and schedule time to monitor the progress you're making with your scheduled tasks.

- Discipline yourself to stick to the scheduled time frames. Going forward, it should be easier to discipline yourself because these time frames will be shorter, less arduous, and more manageable.

Now, it's just a question of better managing the time at your disposal, particularly since unforeseen circumstances could arise at any given moment.

Time Management Strategies

It was all good, and I could soon stop worrying about when I would find the time to do "this, that, and the other." You can too, when you start implementing the following time management strategies (Cope, 2021):

- Even though you may have spent time the previous evening going over what you'd like to do today, your day always begins well with a fresh plan.

- The plan for the day works better once you've psyched yourself up to prioritize your most important tasks, even if it means setting aside the fun things that have stayed at the back of your mind, stubbornly refusing to leave you in peace.

- As I pointed out in the previous section, anything that appears to be large and insurmountable, now needs to be broken down into smaller, manageable chunks. There's less chance of you being discouraged from your plan for the day and deviating from it.

- You also need to cut out as many distractions as possible by creating a clean, safe, and quiet work environment for yourself. It goes without saying that you'll need to place your smart mobile on silent mode and at a safe distance from your work area.

- Forget about trying to multitask. The plan is to complete one task before moving on to the next task.

- Finally, always set aside time to review how your day went. If it didn't go according to plan, you'll at least have an opportunity to try something new without necessarily having to reinvent the wheel.

I can vouch for the efficacy of these strategies because I have tested them, but let me remind you that nothing is achieved overnight, particularly if you're hellbent on rushing through what you've projected you'd like to do. For me, the above strategies could be mastered through a little trial and error. Better still, it could be mastered through the virtuous quality of patience, which too, has taken me time to master.

Setting Deadlines and Timers

Simply put, deadlines need to be realistic. But if you can forgive the pun, the setting of timers doesn't need to be alarming. If you need to set a timer, make sure that the proverbial alarm bell isn't, well, alarming. In my case, I like to use A.I.-inspired birdsong as my wake-up call. It is pleasant to the ear, doesn't distract me, and doesn't even break my concentration at a critical moment of my work.

Techniques for Improving Concentration Levels

Working to schedule, and getting things done on time, is all good and well. But whether less or more is being done, what if the quality of your work is still suffering? What if you're still finding it difficult to concentrate? Go back to my proposed time management strategies, and remind yourself to create the right setting. You can also do the following to help improve your concentration levels (Chia, 2023):

- Practice mindfulness and meditation.

- Learn and choose to focus only on the moment you're in.

- Get more sleep at night, and during the day, continue with the practice of taking short, intermittent breaks, always remembering to keep yourself calm during such moments.

- Do yourself a favor, and connect with nature. Even if it's within your city's public gardens, natural surroundings do a far better job at training your brain to be quiet for a few moments, than sitting in your favorite coffee shop, surrounded by noise.

Going forward, I'd like you to focus on using two techniques that I've found help to keep me calm. Much to my delight, I've discovered that when I'm at my calmest, I am so much more focused.

Meditation

I'm not going to say too much about meditation at this point because that's going to be an integral part of the next chapter where you'll be learning how to manage erratic emotions, find peace and serenity, and learn to keep and stay calm, particularly during the toughest parts of the month.

For me, month ends were always challenging, mainly for two reasons. I had deadlines to meet, and I was always anxious to be paid, not so much so that I could pay my bills on time, but more to do with having money in my pocket so that I could go off and have a good time. It was plain to see that my cluttered mind, if it attempted to focus, tended to focus on things that could be termed a big deal but for the wrong reasons.

How to Create a "Thought Dump"

The second technique I'd like you to try is called a "thought dump." Here's how it works. For starters, you'll need a journal in which you'll record your daily thoughts. But when you do that, the setting in which you'll be for this task needs to be peaceful, quiet, and free of distractions. You'll also need to choose a perfect time of the day for you to achieve this objective (Wisner, 2023).

Now, because you still need to get on with the rest of your day, you'll need to monitor the limited time you have at your disposal to do your thought dumping. It doesn't need to be longer than 10 or 15 minutes. The object of the exercise here is to not let your thoughts run away with you. Previously, I found it too easy to extend my time on a task I enjoyed. It was an easy way out of doing the things that needed to be done (Wisner, 2023).

Finally, don't worry about what you're going to write. Don't worry about untidy handwriting, grammatical errors, or typos. This journal is for your eyes only, and no one else needs to know what you're thinking in those moments (Wisner, 2023).

Strategies for Staying on Task

Today, my strategy is simple, and I'm sure it will work well for you too. As it's still possible that we can easily lose focus and become distracted, we can lose track of the time required to fulfill our tasks.

Of course, there may also be distractions that are not of our own making. So, if for instance, your mom decides to call you for a chat, don't rudely put the phone down on her. Be polite, explaining in no uncertain terms that you still have work to do. Keep your diary handy, making a note of the time spent having a pleasant chat with your mom.

The diary is one of the most important tools you'll need to stay on task. While you meticulously record the daily but manageable tasks that need to be fulfilled, you will also reserve space for a contingency plan in the event that you're steered away from what you're scheduled to do at that particular moment.

What Happens When You Find Things

That Need Your Attention?

I mentioned this earlier, but find myself needing to remind you that you need to learn to prioritize what needs to be done before anything else is attempted. Do this, and you'll soon see how much sooner you get things done. Now that you'll be deliberately attempting this, you'll also see how much more you're able to accomplish.

But what if your mom's call is related to something more urgent? It could be a family crisis that you can hardly ignore. So, when that happens, of course, you'll need to drop what you're doing, and focus on what needs your attention with immediate effect.

This is something that happens all too often in the workplace as well, but when it does, don't panic. Keep calm and safe in the knowledge that the things you wanted to do originally will still get done. You can do this by making use of a functional to-do list.

Creating To-Do Lists With a Notebook or Using Your Mobile
The list is functional because the tasks included are manageable. It's important to note that no matter how much you feel you must do, this list still needs to be kept short. Always bear in mind that there is only so much a person can do in a single day. One critical mistake I have made is being too ambitious and optimistic on how long it takes to do things, and how much I can do in a given timeframe. Needless to say, I now give myself realistic timeframes in my scheduling and play it on the safe side. Plus, trying to adhere to a rigid and fast paced schedule is exhausting.

Finally, it goes without saying that your most important tasks need to be at the top of your list. Even if they're perceptibly easier to do, all other tasks can wait.

If I may, here's a short note on using your phones to record and refer to your to-do lists. Speaking from personal experience, I'd advise against using it at this stage, and recommend using the good-old-fashioned notebook instead. The thing about smartphones is that it's far too close to those social media channels and games you probably like. And no doubt, they'll be whispering in your ear for you to come check them out.

How to Triage Your To-Do List
To make managing your to-do list easier for you, you can do what is known as triage. The following five steps, in the order that they're listed, form the key components of your triage (Springett, 2023):

1. Create a list of the tasks that need to be completed within a specific timeframe.

2. Classify each task in order of its level of urgency and importance.

3. Now, based on these classifications, prioritize the respective tasks based on their level of urgency and importance.

4. Schedule the listed tasks on your calendar in the order that you've prioritized them.

5. Finally, make sure that enough time is allocated to complete each task within the timeframe set.

Always bearing in mind that something new could crop up at an unexpected time, train yourself to be flexible, and always willing to adjust your schedule. Finally, by following the above steps, you'll be able to work more efficiently and effectively, and with less temptation to deliberately distract yourself from what needs to be done (Springett, 2023).

Practicing Minimalism

Before I delve a little deeper into the "less is more philosophy", let me share with you a personal thought, based on my experience of living with ADHD symptoms, both in the past and in the present.

In the past, I had more work to do than I could ever imagine handling. The trouble was, that it was too much to handle, and within a year or so of vain attempts to make as much money as possible, I lost these opportunities. In the process, I also lost my mind.

Fast-forward to the present, and things are looking a lot better. The climb to the top, however, was slow and tentative, and sometimes, even nerve-wracking. Nevertheless, I didn't succumb to the associated pressures, as I did previously, because today, I'm better equipped to handle such pressure, creeping ADHD symptoms notwithstanding. Today, I tend to be a lot more selective over which projects I'd like to take on. And yet, I've succeeded with even *more* work (which I can now handle), and have been able to start putting away savings for a rainy day.

You Only Have so Much You Can Spend in a Day, so Spend It Wisely

Not only have I become an adherent of the "less is more philosophy," I've managed to achieve another objective which entails emphasizing quality over quantity in more ways than one. The quality of the assignments I receive these days is so much better than in the past. And without boasting, the quality of work that I'm producing is better as well. But most importantly–and this is something I really love–the quality of my life has improved immeasurably.

I'm happier, healthier, and I'm seeing other people. It wasn't like that in the past. Time and time again, I failed miserably at relationships as well, and without wishing to cast aspersions on the kind of guys I used to meet, the quality of these men left a lot to be desired as well. It wasn't entirely their fault, mind you.

This, however, is something I'll talk to you about in Chapter 6. For now, though, let's talk about enjoying less, rather than more.

The Less Is More Philosophy

In the past, when my mind was literally everywhere at the same time, I was greedy for more. At some stage in my past life, I even wanted a bigger house, and that too came crashing down like a ton of bricks, metaphorically speaking of course.

Today, however, I live in what others might regard as a tiny apartment. It is a one-bedroom design, but it is free-standing and surrounded by colorful beds of flowers. I have a parking bay, and there is ample parking space for visitors as well. But stepping inside for the first time, visitors might swear that I was living with nothing to my name.

The deception is not intentional, and to be quite honest with you, I quite enjoy the minimalist decor that I've bought into. You see, the less is more philosophy applies to how you live your life as well. There is less clutter. Everything has its place, and is always within reach. And everything you see is aesthetically pleasing as well, and I dare say that given his circumstances back then, this wasn't something that James Joyce could appreciate.

More importantly, "less is more" is good for your personal development. It also simplifies your ability to set goals for yourself. Your daily routines are streamlined, and you are never overwhelmed (Farag, 2023). Finally, I've also managed to achieve the following outcomes by applying the "less is more" philosophy to my life:

- I have more space within which to work.

- I have more time for myself, as well as others.

- I have more energy to do things that I couldn't do before.

- I am not frozen by overwhelming clutter and endless tasks.

Wow! Isn't that awesome? By visualizing and willing yourself to work with less, you end up with more after all. Apply this philosophy to your own life right now, and see where it leads you next. See how it calms you down, and how you become less emotional about everything around you without losing one iota of the empathy for others (and for ourselves!) we've all been born with.

But because of your hyperactive nature and your propensity to easily get distracted, particularly when it feels as though the pressure's about to boil over, you still need to learn how to calm down, stay calm, and manage your emotions better. That's something we'll be looking at in the next chapter.

CHAPTER 5: MANAGING EMOTIONS AND FINDING CALM

No matter how hard I tried, I always found myself lapsing into bouts of impulsivity. But over time, I learned to accept that this was inevitable. I felt like a self-confessed addict going into relapse after many challenging but rewarding weeks on the wagon. Those weeks feel rewarding because one gets to experience what it feels like to be clean and pure, or, in my particular case, "sane."

After doing something about my impulsivity and short span of attention, through self-help deliberations and professionally provided therapy, I experienced what it was like to be calm and keep my emotions in check. So, whenever I have what will forever be known as my down days (thankfully, these are few and far between), I gracefully remind myself that the lapse is temporary, and look forward to the next day.

The next day could always be brighter and better. But then again, you might not need to wait as long as the next day to recover. You could return yourself to calm and serenity within moments of crashing. That's to say that, like me, you will learn how to cope with those symptoms of impulsivity, anxiety, and being overwhelmed which stubbornly refuse to leave you alone.

In this chapter, you're also going to learn to appreciate the virtues of patience. And instead of being your own worst critic, you're going to learn to become your best friend. You'll look forward to spending time alone with yourself. Patience being a good friend of yours as well, you'll look forward to spending time with others once all is said and done as far as priorities are concerned.

You'll look forward to the company of others, even those you couldn't stand or were apprehensive about. Yes, even those you have no alternative but to face during the day, like the rude, gum-chewing sales clerk at the grocery store's checkout counter, or the lazy-good-for-nothing but incredibly loud colleague in the booth next to you at the office.

Coping With Impulsivity, Anxiety, and Being Overwhelmed

Before I run through the things you could do to help you cope with the ADHD symptoms you have on your list, let me quickly talk a little bit more about my symptoms, bearing in mind that, while there may be universal symptoms, there may be one or two areas where we're on opposite sides in terms of how we feel and what we do.

For instance, I have a friend who I met through an ADHD support channel that my therapist had started. While I definitely have my emotional triggers, I can still reign in some of the red-vision rage; depression was my main demon. While my mood can be difficult to shake, especially as of late, the same can not be said of my friend. I watch her go through an emotional roller coaster nearly every time we meet, and if I didn't know about ADHD and what it can feel like, I might not have known how to relate and bring her back to center.

I couldn't have even dreamed of being of any help to her when I was much younger. In fact, I would have followed her on her roller coaster if I hadn't already started to retrain my mind. Part of that is being able to learn how to forgive myself, and also recognizing that I cannot change the world with any number of outbursts or passive aggressive acts. I could, however, change how I reacted and avoid the confrontations and scenarios that occurred regularly, but with different people. Of course, meditation played a role in helping me to be patient as well. Finally, while I regularly assess my behavior these days, I'm not even half as critical of myself as I was back then.

Coping With Impulsivity

If there's one thing I don't do much of these days, it's go to the mall. You see, it's one of the areas that have always tempted the impulsive side of me to lose control. Instead of getting on with grocery shopping, I could be lost in the bookstore, finding four to six volumes for my never shrinking to-be-read pile that I usually don't have the extra money to spend on. I believe the Japanese call this particular habit of buying books and letting them pile up "tsundoku." The fact that there is a term for it somewhere in the world gives me equal measures of relief and aggravation. On the one hand, if there is a term for it, that means it isn't just me. On the other hand, now part of my mind thinks that because it's common enough to have a label, it's fine. My wallet and minimalist decor would like to say it is anything but fine.

Other than reflecting on that blast from the past, I started to do the following to help me cope with my impulsive itches whenever they started to nag me (*Real-World Strategies: "How I Stop Being So Impulsive"*, 2022):

- I stop what I'm about to do and remind myself of the consequences of what I might end up doing.

- I also ask myself why I would want to do something so ridiculous or crazy in the first place.

- I go back to square one and mindfully review the list of things that I should be doing.

- I really don't miss the mall all that much, because I've found better and more pleasurable things to look forward to during my time off for good behavior.

- Finally, if I do go out to do some shopping, I never do it alone. I let my shopping companion know how much I am willing to spend and on what, and they hold my card for the duration of our trip. (A note on finding a shopping companion, make sure you can trust them and that they are not as impulsive as you).

Coping With Hyperactivity

I think one of the reasons why I've managed to reduce my hyperactivity symptoms drastically, compared to other ADHD sufferers, is that I was able to embrace exercise and physical activities like a duck to water. I've always been active. Even on my worst days when I could no longer keep my backside on my chair to do serious work, I'd whip around the house I used to rent with my vacuum cleaner, dusters, carpet cleaner, cleaning detergents, brushes, and sponges.

To be sure, things would get done (or partially done) around the house, but alas, nary a thing got done at my desk. Anyway, physical stimulation remains one of the best ways to help you cope with hyperactivity. It can also help you to relieve yourself of stress, calm your mind, and work off the excess energy that your hyperactive moods have produced (Smith, 2023).

It's a lot healthier for you to spend time outdoors doing your exercise, and yes, you don't need to spend hours indoors doing housework. Furthermore, it helps if you have a partner or two to exercise with. It's great being able to surround yourself with good, influential friends who help take your mind off the things that have been causing you to become hyperactive in the first place (Smith, 2023).

Finally, exercise, accompanied by a healthy diet, acts as a

counterweight against your ADHD symptoms which, if left unchecked, can have a detrimental effect on your health. But the key to staying healthy is to exercise regularly (Smith, 2023).

My go to exercises have been swimming, dancing, and qi gong. Up until I stopped having a gym membership, swimming was one of my favorite things to do. Ballroom dancing is a close second and has definitely become the one that burns the most energy and generally is the most fun for me. Qi gong is my daily evening exercise to help me stretch out strained muscles and help me achieve a calmer state of mind. What exercises would you be interested in trying?

Managing Stress and Anxiety

Of course, you're not going to be able to destress if you're sweating it out on something that you're clearly not enjoying. So, if you like being around people, you could join a club and take up a sport you've enjoyed watching on TV. But if you like spending quality time alone like me, a good walk in the park or woods could be just what you need for your mental well-being (Smith, 2023).

Even time spent sitting on a park bench for half an hour at a time will do wonders for bringing you stress relief. The key here is that you're surrounded by sunshine and greenery, both of which are very good for reducing stress and anxiety symptoms which, unfortunately, are two further symptoms of ADHD. You might also want to try your hand at yoga, qi gong or tai chi. These disciplines are known to help teach ADHD sufferers how to gain control over their emotions and impulses (Smith, 2023).

Yoga and tai chi can, however, require you to join a class. You could buy DVDs, or stream videos on how to do these exercises, but it doesn't quite replace the benefits of having an experienced teacher to not only get the full benefits of the exercises, but also keep you from accidentally harming yourself. You need to be able to do the practices 100% effectively if you want to derive full benefit from them.

Meditation, on the other hand, could be self-taught if you're prepared to discipline yourself to sit or stand still for just 10 minutes at a time. There are hundreds of videos and apps that offer guided meditations if you are unsure about how to start, or need help getting into a focused mindset.

The key to learning how to meditate is to be patient and forgiving of yourself. Many people call the untrained mind, the "monkey mind" because it is easily distracted and goes off on its own to curiously follow its fixation. It's not just people with ADHD who struggle with it, though; almost every untrained mind is like this. We sit down to be still, and the mind is anything but. This is where it is so important to be forgiving. If we chastise ourselves or harshly tell ourselves to be still, meditation becomes stressful and unpleasant. Instead, acknowledge that the mind wandered, and gently tell our mind that while that is an interesting thought, it can be something to think of after meditation. Be grateful of seeing the clouds in the sky, but don't follow them to the horizon. See the cloud, then let it pass as you look back at the sky. What I mean is, after you discover your mind wandered, gently say it's time to go back and focus on counting your breaths.

Another thing I enjoy about meditation is that it can be done anywhere. So, let me introduce you to no more than two basic meditation exercises that you can try out at home without any supervision.

The First Meditation You'll Do to Calm Yourself Down

Let's face it, ADHD sufferers stress a lot, don't they? And when you stress, your breath is a lot shallower than it should be. So, it makes sense that your first-ever meditation is a breathing meditation. The breathing meditation teaches you to breathe deeply, particularly when you're feeling that you need to run off and do something crazy. Do this meditation once a day in the morning, and you should start to feel more peaceful and calm throughout the rest of the day (Riopel, 2019).

So, start by breathing in through your nose for no more than four seconds, and then hold your breath for another seven seconds. After that, exhale through your mouth for about eight seconds. You probably won't start to destress straight after this cycle, so repeat it at least three times. But if, for some reason, you start to feel dizzy after the first or second cycle, stop what you're doing, and come back the following morning and try the meditation again when you're feeling a little stronger (Riopel, 2019).

Help Yourself Focus With Another Meditation

Because losing your focus is a regular symptom of ADHD, it makes sense to try doing a focus meditation as well. Rest assured that this meditation is both easy and fun to do. The fun part of the meditation requires you to focus on anything in your room or within your outdoor surroundings that happens to be of particular interest to you (Riopel, 2019).

Indoors, I like to whip out some paints and focus on what I'm attempting to convey, or I'll just sit and observe one of my houseplants. I'll look at every leaf, see every branch, and take note of every pattern and scent. Outdoors, it's the colors of the sunflowers outside my living room window that attract my attention, like their pollen would a few bees in the neighborhood. The object of the exercise is to select anything that is likely to stimulate your senses. So, if you like roses or a bottle of red wine, take as much time as you like staring at the object of your desire, imagining what it would feel like if you touched it, or taste like if you should want to taste it (Riopel, 2019).

The focus meditation requires you to zero in on the details of the object in front of you to the point that, after a few seconds, you don't see or notice anything else. The meditation will help you deepen your focus while you hold your attention (Riopel, 2019).

I can't wait for you to tell me just how effective this meditation exercise was for you. By the way, there will be space provided for you at the end of this book to tell me how you feel about the tools I've provided for you.

Focusing on One Thing At a Time

One thing at a time, because you still need to learn how to forgive yourself. Forgiveness may be one important requirement for your well-being, but just think for a moment about what it will achieve for you in the future. To my mind, if you're able to forgive yourself, you're patient with yourself. Speaking of which, you will have learned to be patient with the world around you.

Attitude is Nearly Everything

Our attitudes don't just help shape the world we live in, they can color how we see everything. It's more than just optimism or pessimism, it's if we are open or timid, domineering or benevolent, flippant or serious, ungrateful or appreciative. I can't think of a scenario in which any extreme of these attitudes is truly beneficial, but having a healthy mix and seeing through the right lens at the right time can be the difference between starting an exciting new adventure, missing an opportunity, or going into a certain disaster. With the wrong attitude, a great opportunity can turn into a huge mistake, but with the right attitude, a huge mistake can become a life changing, golden opportunity.

There are actually two bits of Chinese wisdom that I would like to draw upon to help illustrate my point. I gleaned both of these from the delightful works of Benjamin Hoff, *The Tao of Pooh* and *The Te of Piglet*. If you haven't read either of these gems, I highly recommend them. Reading these books definitely helped me in changing the way I not only saw the world, but how I acted and reacted to it. Now, to the actual wisdom:

The first is the famous painting subject of the three vinegar tasters. One taster was a buddhist, who had a bitter expression. He saw the world as an endless cycle of rebirth and suffering until Nirvana was reached. The second taster was a confucianist, who wore a sour expression. In Confucianism, perfection is prioritized and is the only way to achieve peace and harmony. The last taster was a taoist, who saw that things were the way they were supposed to be, and he could appreciate things for how they were. He was the only one of the three pictured as smiling (Hoff, 1982, p. 2).

This can be applied to how we go into different situations or view things in our daily lives. If we go in with a constantly negative attitude or predetermined idea of what things should be, then it is almost like a self-fulfilling prophecy. We will be rewarded with disappointment, bitterness, and sorrow. However, if we adopt an attitude that is more open and curious, we can have a greater appreciation.

The other bit of wisdom is the parable of the farmer and his horse. In this parable, an old farmer lived with his son, and they had only one horse. One day, the horse ran away. The neighbors came to commiserate and said, "What bad luck!" The old man merely said, "Maybe it is, maybe it isn't."

The next day, the horse returned with an entire herd. The son corralled them, and the neighbors came back to congratulate the old man, saying, "What great luck!" to which the old man replied, "We'll see."

When the son tried to break in one of the horses, it bucked him off and he broke his leg. The neighbors again came to say how unlucky this was. The old man again replied, "Maybe it's bad, maybe it's good. Who can tell?"

A short time later, the imperial army came through and took every able bodied young man in the village with them to fight a war far away. Almost none of the young men were ever seen again. However, the old farmer's son was spared because of his broken leg (Hoff, 1992, p. 171).

We can't see if things will really be bad or good. Our attitudes really determine a lot of that, as well as our level of success and happiness. The rest is chance.

You are Your Own Worst Critic

Being hypercritical of yourself and your actions gets you nowhere. But no harm is done to your well-being when you're able to utilize your newly acquired forgiving nature to reflect on the mistakes you've made. This is what it means to self-reflect, and how else are you going to be able to learn from your past mistakes if you aren't prepared to review them?

The final chapter of this book contains a section that will demonstrate how you can self-reflect productively without losing any sleep over how the exercise makes you feel afterwards. If anything, you will start to feel better in the long run.

Learning to Forgive Yourself

One of the best ways you can start learning to forgive yourself is by learning to love yourself. This wise piece of advice came to me from the most unlikely source, back when my ADHD was spinning out of control, so much so that I was as miserable as sin.

I was never much of a jazz fan back then (I am today), but it was George Benson's song *The Greatest Love of All* that struck a chord with me. Only the thing is, he wasn't singing. It was the lovely Whitney Houston's voice that brought a tear to my eye. It wasn't love at the first sound, but it got me thinking anyway.

You Can Be Patient With the World Around You

By now, I'm sure you can relate to most of what I've been telling you about myself since the beginning of this book. You know exactly what I mean when I tell you that I couldn't seem to sit still for five minutes. You also know what it feels like to be impatient when things aren't going your way.

And when that happens, you also know that not only do you act on impulse, you sometimes take your frustrations out on others. And when *that* happens, it's usually the people closest to you that you hurt the most. That would also explain why I wasn't good at holding down a steady relationship for more than five months at a time, if it ever came to that.

But never mind that, because in the next chapter, we're going to talk about what it takes to get on with others, particularly those who are close to us.

CHAPTER 6: NAVIGATING RELATIONSHIPS

I wasn't always an introvert with social anxiety. When I was very young, my mother loved to parade me around because I was apparently quite charming and well-behaved. It seemed like I could make friends with anyone I came across. Then one day, seemingly out of nowhere, I started to hide behind my mother when we went out. I chose the shy attitude instead of my former bold demeanor. Little by little, it became worse and worse. I had to be reminded to smile and laugh. My mother almost gave up on me, and began to resort to bullying to get me out of the house. As time went by, the social skills that were just developing began to deteriorate. I would get flustered and my filter went out the window. Then as I began to put my foot in my mouth more and more, I offended more people, and I became even more withdrawn. The me in middle school up until my early thirties was an awkward, easily flustered, easily frustrated, wallflower. I wish I could say I was joking when half of my high school was rocked by the knowledge that I wasn't mute during my senior year.

I didn't make many friends. In fact, I was very good at pushing people away, especially the ones I actually wanted in my life. I look back on those times now and cringe. I still don't have many friends, but that's because I'm happily ensconced in my home and have become quite the workaholic. Add to that that everyone I used to know has moved on with their lives, either moving far away, or getting married and starting families. It also doesn't help that I live in a city that doesn't offer much for singles on budgets. Don't get me wrong, I might not have a large social circle, but I can get along with almost anyone I meet now and have some decent conversations. Even when I was a manager in my last job, I was able to get along with most of the associates, and have difficult conversations when necessary. Confrontations were no longer out of my control, nor were they terrifying.

What could possibly have been the catalyst that transformed me from someone incapable of connecting with people to someone able to converse with anyone of my choosing?

Communicating Effectively, Building Support Systems, and Managing Conflict

I doubt if we'll ever be with the right partner for us if we still don't communicate effectively. It won't help much either if we don't get out much, preferring to hide away from folks in order to avoid conflict. Don't worry, because if I can learn to manage conflict when it occurs, then so can you.

Today, the same old rude, gum-chewing sales clerk is still at the checkout counter where I usually do my grocery shopping. But I gave up wondering why the store manager never moved her to the back of the store, out of plain sight of budget-stressed shoppers, because today, I'm able to take her impertinence in my stride. It's on her if she wants to behave poorly in front of customers, and I think by now, she's grown up enough to know better. After all, we can't change the way the majority of the world goes about doing something that annoys us, much as we try. All we can do is plan accordingly, and do our best to change how we react to the world. that little nugget of wisdom actually came to me one day when I was still working as a clerk. It dawned on me as I was about to get frustrated for the umpteenth time about something nearly everyone did, that it wasn't their job to know what annoyed me or how things worked in this particular store. It was MY job. Becoming antagonistic and passive aggressive with nearly every guess when they did the thing that drove me nuts wasn't going to change everyone who came in. It would, however, drive away the very people who were the source of my paychecks.

I'd like to add a sober reminder that we're not supermen or women. We can't single-handedly change the world. We're also not invincible, and if that's really the case, it helps to be able to depend on someone trustworthy who could potentially help us during our moments of weakness or if we find ourselves up against someone domineering.

How to Communicate Effectively

Rest assured that it doesn't require rocket science to communicate effectively. For you, it could just be a question of being able to make eye contact with the person in front of you, and reading his non-verbal cues. You can also use the following strategies to help you communicate better with folks, whether it's the irritating sales clerk downtown or the hulky nightclub bouncer scaring you witless with his intimidating stare (Gattig, 2023):

- Always take into account what kind of person you're dealing with and the environment you are encountering them in.

- Don't ramble or stutter when just a polite, confident one-liner will probably do it for you.

- If you know you're meeting someone beforehand, prepare yourself to deliver the best message possible. It's okay to practice talking in front of a mirror, but this is probably best done in the privacy of your home.

- After you've initiated the face-to-face communication, encourage the receiver of your message to reciprocate.

- Once the conversation or discussion is over, it's not a bad idea to ask for feedback.

This can even be utilized for the workplace. Even if your employer's dissatisfaction with your reasonable excuse for being late at your desk in the morning is inherently unreasonable or unfair, it helps to know where you stand in order to protect yourself.

How to Build Support Systems

In terms of building a support system that works in your favor, there are numerous avenues you could explore. You would be required to choose one, perhaps even two, avenues that resonate directly with your circumstances and the state you're in. Whichever support group you decide to join must make you feel welcome, so much so that you look forward to returning for the next meeting.

It also helps to be in the company of like-minded folks who are dealing with similar ADHD symptoms. But if that's the case, it's best that your support group is led by a qualified therapist or caregiver authorized to provide you and your fellow group members with care, support, and advice.

Can you imagine hanging out with a group of people who are all vulnerable, and not being monitored or supervised? Instead of healing, folks could run riot, metaphorically speaking. If not that, they may be hesitant to open up in front of strangers, particularly if it's the first time they're attending a group session.

Online or social media-aligned support groups need to be approached with caution, and it's probably in your best interest to join a network that has been approved or recommended by a mental health organization or group of therapists.

Finally, family support is a good idea as well. Moreover, it would be ideal that each closely-knit family member has been consulted by your therapist as well. This allows them to have a better understanding of your condition, and respond positively and constructively should you ever be engaged in a crisis, whether it's personal or work-related.

Managing Conflict

Conflict resolution usually applies to the workplace. It also applies to family settings, particularly when arguments and disagreements arise. Successful and well-adjusted folks are usually adept at managing conflict. But speaking from experience, I see no reason why people with ADHD can't handle conflict as well as the next person. Granted, a little extra TLC will need to be applied. In the meantime, the following tips should help you on your way (*Tips for Managing Conflict*, (n.d.):

- Accept that conflict in life is inevitable.

- Learn not just to calm yourself down, but learn to calm the other party involved in the conflict down as well.

- While listening actively to what your antagonist or complainant has to say, analyze the conflict that arose.

- When responding in kind, try your best to utilize neutral language.

- While agreeing that you and your opponent will work together as a team from now on, it's permissible that you both agree to disagree.

- It is more than okay to call a temporary time-out when things get too heated and take a five to ten minute breather.

The most critical thing to remember in any conversation is the reason why most people become frustrated. The bottom line is that everyone wants to feel understood. As long as you show that you are understanding, or at least trying to understand, where the other person is coming from, you can avoid a knock-down, drag-out argument. In fact, it makes it easier to find a peaceable agreement.

This approach to conflict can be applied anywhere, but especially at work. The work environment would be wholly ineffective if its leader was surrounded by proverbial yes-men, so it is important to be able to get many ideas out without doing more than ruffling feathers. Let's be honest, not only would life be boring if we all agreed on everything, we'd become pretty stagnant.

Navigating Social Situations With ADHD

As an ADHD sufferer, having to weave your way around and through social situations is probably one of the most challenging aspects of your life. Being used to working in isolation for most of my waking hours, was particularly challenging for me, even at the best of times. We've also had to resign ourselves to the fact that there are some things about ourselves that we simply cannot change.

However, that doesn't mean that we need to suffer. It doesn't mean that others need to be irritated or disarmed by our quirks, either. Having said that, we always need to monitor our facial expressions, tone of voice, and body language, over and above our general behavior, alongside training ourselves to focus on how others perceive us (Mandriota, 2022).

When in the company of others, we also need to be mindful of the following (Mandriota, 2022):

- dominating a conversation
- interrupting or talking over others
- jumping from one subject to the next
- talking about unrelated or inappropriate subjects

Finally, what makes life (positively) interesting for ADHD sufferers is that we're always curious, enthusiastic, passionate, and interesting to others. Well, most of the time anyway (Mandriota, 2022).

Improving Communication With Loved Ones

Isn't life interesting? In my case, of all the things I have in common with my mother, it's ADHD, previously known as ADD (attention deficit disorder). And to add insult to injury, our incessant need to talk at the same time is really irritating to my dad, even at the best of times.

I remember one occasion when my mom, being quite ill at the time, was close to tears, complaining that as the family matriarch, she was never given a chance to talk. So, with two male siblings rivaling me for our parents' attention, I was not alone after all. During my mom's outburst back then, I was taken aback, and as I walked out the back door, getting ready to leave for my tiny apartment, I jested that the next time I returned for an obligatory visit, I would bring a roll of masked tape.

I would tape my mouth shut in case I couldn't keep it shut while someone else was talking. I was able to laugh at my disability, but seriously, though, I knew that I had to learn to listen intently while patiently waiting for an opportunity to speak. This afterthought would become particularly pertinent for me when in the company of those who were senior to me.

Improving Communication With Coworkers

In the workplace, it would be important for me to look and listen before speaking. I still have to practice this discipline because today, working from home as I do, I rarely need to attend meetings, whether one-on-one or in a group.

Of course, these days, effective communication with coworkers or peers is of equal importance to the online environment as well. It might not even be a video call, it could just as well be a live messaging session. So, when this happens, I'll practice what I call a mini-meditation session while patiently waiting my turn to message. By the way, this meditation is an abbreviated version of the breathing meditation I introduced to you in the previous chapter.

But it's easier said than done for the ADHD-afflicted team member. What if there's a narcissist or bully in our midst as well? To my mind, the onus rests with the manager, supervisor, team or group leader, or initiator of this meeting, whether viral or in person, to chair the meeting to ensure that everyone remains on board in equal measure. Of course, in this setting, a little scheduling or list-making wouldn't hurt either.

When Conflict Happens

Quite frankly, it's no use hiding away from people, or zigzagging sideways, left and right, like a timid beach crab, always trying to avoid a potential conflict. Whether we like it or not, conflict is part of life. Heck, if victims of narcissistic abuse can learn to handle conflict, then so can we. But how to go about it as a lifetime ADHD sufferer, therein lies the rub.

Pick and Choose Your Battles

I think it's safe to say that in an imperfect world, not of our making (we're all peace lovers, right?), we have to reconcile ourselves to be selective when taking on issues that are important to us, and have the potential to evolve into a heated debate or, worse still, an abusive argument. It's in our best interests, not only to safeguard our mental well-being, but to ensure that our loved ones are emotionally and physically safe as well.

So, in my line of work, I've replaced my previously bad reputation for bravado and braggadocio with good-old-fashioned bravery in order to ensure that I remain unbiased, impartial, and non-confrontational when discussing or debating work-related matters. Indeed, in my case, talking to a religious zealot about treating gender dysphoria sufferers with empathy and care remains challenging.

Staying Calm

I'm not going to say much about staying calm at this point, except to refer you to the two previous chapters on keeping yourself organized and mentally well. My argument remains that if we can be better organized in spite of our ADHD difficulties, there'll be less chance of us spinning into a spiral of panic attacks when things get a little hot in the kitchen.

And no, I'm not an advocate of the pessimistic adage that suggests that if we can't stand the heat in the kitchen, then we must leave it. No! Let's deal with it, rather. This book's final two chapters will provide you with further organizational tools, as well as health-oriented advice, that will equip you well to keep calm and just carry on, as the famous British adage would have you know.

The Five-Minute Cooldown

It might not be convenient for you to meditate at your desk. After all, your antagonist might even think that you're sleeping on the job. It might not even be possible to do a walking meditation outdoors. The same antagonist might think that you're shirking. So, do this instead. Go to the bathroom. Quietly close and lock your cubicle door, seat yourself (make sure the seat's clean and sanitized first), and do your calming-down meditation, right there and then.

After all, when nature calls, we've all got to go some time, and who's going to stop you, right?

All About Conflict Resolution

While conflict remains unavoidable, even at the best of times, conflict resolution is *always* possible. Based on the extensive research I've done over the last few years, from South Africa's Truth and Reconciliation Commission, spearheaded by Archbishop Emeritus Desmond Tutu (ideas on what to do during a major conflict) to the infamous 2016 and 2020 US Presidential Election debates, spearheaded by former U.S. President Donald Trump (ideas on what *not* to do during a major conflict), all I can say is that there are numerous ways in which we can, potentially, resolve conflicts peacefully and amicably.

But given that we may be more vulnerable than most folks around us, we still need to exercise care and caution. So, before I close this chapter, let me propose that you learn to do any one or more of the following (*5 Conflict Resolution Strategies We All Use*, 2016):

- Avoid conflict altogether.

- Defeat conflict when you've got your back against the proverbial wall.

- Compromise during a conflicting situation.

- Accommodate your antagonist in order to appease him or get him to leave you alone.

- Collaborate with your antagonist, instead of arguing with him, to come up with amicable solutions.

- Get what military drill instructors and drill sergeants refer to as a "Battle Buddy," not so much to do actual battle, but to have your back, and worst case scenario, act as a witness or mediator.

Sometimes, it feels better to find someone who is stronger than you emotionally, someone you can trust to help you out of a difficult situation. Drama and conflicts happen often enough in the workplace, and rather than grab the bull by the horns, many of us choose to stay uncharacteristically quiet and tough it out, in order to safeguard our jobs.

As I found out in the past, attempting to stay "strong and silent", or quietly keeping a low profile, far away from potential potboilers, doesn't always work. You can run a mile from conflict situations but as Murphy's Law would have it, conflict usually has a nasty habit of catching up with you, particularly when you haven't addressed your inner emotional turmoil.

A famous quote by Sun Tzu goes, "Know yourself, know your enemies, and you will not need to fear the result of a thousand battles." If you understand who you are dealing with and how they usually react, what they want, what their strengths and weaknesses are, and what they have at their disposal, then that is half the battle. However, that won't do you much good if you don't know what bothers you, what motivates you, what you are capable of, and what can be used against you. It takes a bit of introspection, which meditation can help with, to achieve a good understanding of how you think and why. Once armed with that knowledge, not only can you better understand others, but you can also heal some of your own mental wounds and help facilitate positive change.

Honestly, entire books can be written about conflict resolution and navigating social situations, and they are in print. In this chapter, I've given you advice and knowledge that has worked for me. However, it might not work as well for you. While I still encourage you to give it your best try, I think further reading wouldn't hurt to help deepen your understanding. My favorite works on the topic that I highly recommend are *How to Win*

Friends and Influence People by Dale Carnegie, and *The Laws of Human Nature* by Robert Greene.

So, now we are armed with the basics of how to not just cope with, but begin to enjoy social situations. Next, not only are you going to learn how to deal with conflict in the workplace, but you're going to be motivated to find the right job that allows you to thrive, ADHD or no ADHD.

CHAPTER 7: CAREER SUCCESS WITH ADHD

I'm very happy with the direction my career has taken me. Earlier, I mentioned how I used to scramble for work, and I highlighted how I hunted down new assignments for the wrong reasons. On those occasions that I did find jobs that paid well, I ended up not enjoying them. For one thing, the subjects that I was tasked to write about were too commercially-oriented for my liking.

Inevitably, it made no difference whether I was paid handsomely or not. I derived no job satisfaction, and I was always miserable. But once I managed to get my ADHD symptoms under control, I experienced a remarkably positive turnaround. I did not necessarily land assignments that one would usually define as dream jobs in the commercial sense. The new assignments I was awarded were providing me not only with job satisfaction, but a sense of self-worth as well.

Not only was the work helping me, it was helping others, too. And today, here we are. I'm a certified bibliotherapist, widely recognized for my ability to write with empathy and responsibility, bearing in mind that many of my readers' states of mind may have been vulnerable at the time of reading my material.

At the end of this book, there's a reference page you can refer to, should you ever wish to extend your reading on your ADHD symptoms, and how best to deal with them.

Finding the Right Job, Thriving in the Workplace, and Achieving Goals

If it hasn't already happened to you in the past as well, I'd like you to avoid finding a job for the wrong reasons. And in case you've already forgotten what I said earlier about my ill-begotten motivations, it might surprise you to learn that sometimes in life, we need to stop focusing on work that pays the most money.

Shouldn't our common sense already be telling us that the more a job pays, the more likely it will be that we could be overburdened with the work we're tasked to do? And, when that happens, you could be faced with burnout, unable to haul in your featured ADHD symptoms that continue to run a mile from you at a world-record pace. Also, you surely won't be happy in a job like this, right?

Identifying Your Strengths and Finding the Right Job Fit

So, isn't it more important to find something that you know you'll enjoy? It doesn't matter if there's pressure or not. Pressure is a fact of life anyway, and it's just a matter of learning how to cope with it. The way a friend of mine put it to me once, "Just pick your favorite flavor of sh*t-sandwich." In his own crude way, he went on to explain that even if you land your dream job, there will still be something about it that will make it less than perfect, be it the pay, the people, or the tasks. It could be as stupid as hating the commute or lunch options. You have to be realistic and find a job that you like best, and can learn to live with whatever you don't like about it.

Also, it makes common sense to find something that you're good at. This, however, doesn't mean that you'll be taking on a job as a taxi driver just because you're an excellent driver. It could just be that you're very good with people, and if you're driving a cab every day, you're going to bump into a lot of people every day anyway, right?

So, before you go job hunting, make a list of your strengths. At the same time, it makes sense to note your weaknesses as well so that you can address them too.

If you don't already know what type of career you wish to pursue, that's okay. I probably wouldn't have even thought about becoming a writer if I hadn't taken a few career aptitude quizzes. I've found some to be more helpful than others, simply because they weren't particularly accurate. Some, however, pointed me in the right direction once I was completely honest in my answers and tried not to fish for a particular outcome.

If you already have a career that you know you wish to pursue, then finding the right work environment for you to thrive will be the biggest focus. You'll have to really research the place you are thinking of working at. If there is something about it that would make you absolutely dread the day, then keep looking. Red flags would include a high employee turnover rate, poor associate satisfaction ratings on help-wanted websites, and if the work environment itself causes discomfort or concern when you visit or go in for an interview.

Something to remember about interviews is that while they are interviewing you to see if they want to bring you onboard, you must also be interviewing them to see if their company is the right fit for you. Granted, if you're getting a job out of desperation, or just finding something to get you through until you can land your dream job, it might seem wise to overlook things at first. However, you might be at that job indefinitely, so if you are not careful, you could be stuck in a job that is detrimental to your mental, or even physical, health for weeks, months, or years. If you wish to thrive and not merely survive, you have to be discerning about where and with whom you will be spending the majority of your waking hours.

Excelling in the Workplace with ADHD

Ultimately, I believe you can excel. That's to say that you apply a similar attitude of fortitude and diligence as you would to addressing your daily behavior in order to ensure that ADHD and its ingratiating symptoms don't get the better of you.

For instance, if you're chatting via a mobile or landline, you'll take notes to make sure that you haven't missed what your fellow conversationalist has said. This also helps you to keep paying attention, and it's a generally accepted business practice to take notes during meetings anyway (Watson, 2022).

Workwise, you'll still be scheduling and making to-do lists. Of course, it goes without saying that you'll need to train and discipline yourself to stay organized during your workday. Careerwise, you'll have goals, but will need to ensure that they're realistic at all times (Watson, 2022).

Finding the Right Goal Strategy for You

It's great to have goals in mind. But it's discouraging to always be distracted from these goals, never being able to reach them. That said, here are a few ways to help get you on the correct path that helps bring you closer to achieving the realistic goals you've set for yourself (Walsh, 2022):

- First and foremost, you always need to ask yourself why you want to achieve these goals.

- Not only must your goals be realistic if you're ever going to be able to achieve them, they must be meaningful, and connected to the reason why you want to achieve them.

- Your goals can be purposeful as well if they're connected to your priorities in life.

- Use your ability to hyper-focus and set your focus on your goals. By doing that, you'll be striving to eliminate all other distractions that currently stand in your way.

- Build an understanding and appreciation of what's most important in your life and career. This will also help you to create clarity and meaning for the goals you've set for yourself.

- But before you even think of achieving your goals, make sure that you've removed the obstacles that could impede you from achieving them.

What Helps You Stay Motivated?

I must admit that money is still a common denominator for me. This may have something to do with the trauma I experienced in the past from not having money. But without much input from my therapists, I've been able to put money at the back of my mind by always thinking about what my clients are going to be getting from the work I produce for them.

And no, they're not going to be making lots of money from my effort. The publishing business, as it exists right now, is cutthroat and competitive. No, our thoughts are with the folks that will be reading our books. If our words can make a positive, meaningful impact on their lives, then we've done our work well.

So, what, then, helps to keep you motivated? You can help yourself answer this question by making notes in your journal.

Finding Balance

You'll have a better chance of career fulfillment once you've been able to find the right balance between your work and your personal life. Having an equal amount of time for both work and life could be richly rewarding. But it could be even more enriching if you're able to enjoy the things that tug at your heartstrings the most. Having said that, you'll still need to make sure that you don't get carried away with your impulses. And you can do that by making sure that you're able to avoid burnout, and take better care of yourself.

Avoiding Burnout

Burnout is serious, and it needs to be avoided at all costs. How and why is it serious? If you succumb to burnout, you could be flat on your back for weeks, metaphorically. Then again, it's not unknown for some folks who have suffered from the syndrome to actually be confined to their beds, whether they simply felt they couldn't move a muscle out of bed or were prescribed bed rest by their medical practitioners.

So, to effectively reduce the chances of you succumbing to burnout as a consequence of your ADHD behavior, it's essential that you first understand and appreciate what burnout is. For starters, burnout is usually related to work-related stress. You'll know you're on the verge of burnout when you're exhausted and have run out of energy.

What Is Burnout?

Burnout is defined as a state of complete mental, physical, and emotional exhaustion. If you have burnout, you'll find it difficult to engage in meaningful activities in similar ways you would if overwhelmed by your ADHD-related impulses. Apart from feeling hopeless, you sometimes couldn't care less what happens to you, let alone to others (*Signs you might be experiencing a burnout and how to regain balance in your life*, 2021).

Other than that, the following are five significant signs that you could be heading towards burnout (*Signs you might be experiencing a burnout and how to regain balance in your life*, 2021):

- headaches
- stomach aches
- fatigue
- frequent illness
- loss of appetite
- a lack of sleep

How to Overcome Burnout When It Happens

Earlier, I spoke about the importance of achieving balance. Once you've done that, chances are good that you could avoid suffering from burnout. But if you should be heading towards a burnout crash, you can do the following to pull back the symptoms (*Signs you might be experiencing a burnout and how to regain balance in your life*, 2021):

- Take another look at the way you're working. Reexamine your home life, and then strive to find new meaning, value, and balance.

- You'll also need to take another look at your priorities. Doing so may even allow you a pleasant break or two away from those things that would have usually distracted you, or caused you stress.

- Seek a healthy outlet for your impulses by feeding your

creative instincts, and doing something that really interests you.

- Remind yourself again that being physically active, enjoying a healthy diet, and a good night's rest are integral to your overall mental well-being.

Spend more time reading before and after you've done your journal exercises. This allows you to think more reflectively about what you're doing, what you'd like to do, your current circumstances, and your current state of health. It will feed you with fresh ideas on how to improve your life by creating a healthy, balanced work/life regime that is unique to what you aspire to, and who you are as a human being.

The next chapter will help you to become more constructive and organized in lieu of creating that easy-to-follow plan.

CHAPTER 8: BUILDING HABITS FOR LONG-TERM SUCCESS

It is all good and well that you've now managed to get used to new routines, and successfully set goals for yourself. But what if these routines are work-related? What if these goals are linked to your long-term career aspirations? And what if the schedules you've created are related to how well you're taking care of your family while managing your ADHD symptoms?

It's fair to suggest that the creation of routines, and the setting of goals, needs to be carried out with a great deal of care. Not only are you accountable to yourself, you're accountable to others as well. Getting used to new, healthy habits can help keep you accountable and sustainable, priming you for long-term success and beating task paralysis.

The difference between mental paralysis and task paralysis is that mental paralysis is more like sensory overload and your mind and body just say, "Nope." You could be in the middle of a grocery store, and suddenly feel like you can't go a step further because there's just too much going on around you and in your own mind. Task paralysis is when you are overwhelmed by your to-do list, as task that you aren't sure how to go about doing, or you feel like you have to wait for the perfect conditions to complete the task and so you just can't bring yourself to even begin. I can still hear my siblings in the back of my mind scoffingly call me lazy whenever this set in.

In either case, I've found something that works for me to help me get moving again. For me, panic feels very similar to when I am overwhelmed, possibly because panic is such an overwhelming feeling. I treat it the same way I do when I go on a run and start to feel short of breath.

My thoughts begin to race in a negative direction and scream at me to stop and gasp for breath. I've merely lost my cadence. So, without stopping, I look at where I am going, close my eyes for a moment and take a very deep breath, hold it, and let it out slowly. Then I get back into my breathing rhythm and it's like the panic never happened.

I apply that same deep breath when there is too much going on at once, or I have no idea where to start. I close my eyes and stop my thoughts to focus on that deep breath. After I've let it out, I am ready to triage and tackle with renewed vigor. It's almost like hitting a reset button.

Worst case scenario, if I am really struggling with an overwhelming task list, I call in for some help, either to delegate a few things, or to help show me how to do something I am unsure about. It also helps that I have learned to accept that conditions will never be perfect to get anything done, so it's best to make a plan, then hold yourself to it and start when you say you will. Ask that person you called in for help to keep you accountable if necessary. There's no shame in calling in for assistance. On the contrary, it's actually popular, sound advice.

Creating Routines, Setting Goals, and Staying Accountable

I mentioned in an earlier chapter that before I addressed my ADHD symptoms, I perceived routine to be a boring enterprise. I didn't, however, say that the setting of goals was always something I derived a lot of excitement from. The problem, though, was that these goals would usually overwhelm me. They weren't realistic, either. I also lacked motivation to follow through on my routines, but once the wellbeing of others was at stake, I became a little more motivated to succeed.

Initially, it did put pressure on me, but thanks to being able to follow a daily but flexible routine, I was able to pull through. You see, routines become more manageable when you follow through on them in the priority order you've set. Finally, you can make being accountable a little easier on your shoulders when you involve others to help monitor your progress.

How to Prioritize Tasks and Responsibilities

To help you better prioritize your tasks, you could make use of what is known as SMART goal setting. This will be summarized below. In the meantime, work towards prioritizing what your mom and dad may have inculcated in you as your daily responsibilities.

This, of course, may entail having to take care of other people's needs alongside your own, just as long as the demands placed on you are reasonable, and you're able to avoid burning yourself out, something I showed you how to do at the end of the previous chapter. Having said that, it's vitally important that you take good care of yourself, before taking care of others. This, however, is not selfishness. It's just plain common sense. After all, if you're not able to take care of yourself, how are you going to take care of your responsibilities towards others? As the saying goes, you can't pour from an empty cup.

Hold Yourself Accountable by Asking Others to Help

Holding yourself accountable has another angle. It's interesting to see human nature in action. We have a tendency to do what we're supposed to do, or what is expected of us, when we're aware that others are watching us or monitoring us. This is probably one of the salient reasons why it's been so difficult for many folks to adjust to working from home, post-COVID-19.

No one's watching them, right? And particularly when you're as tired as a dog, the TV couch or bed always looks so inviting. I can use my interaction with my dad as a touching example of holding myself accountable. Come to think of it, it was my dad's idea. I had just emerged from my worst-ever ADHD crisis, and naturally, it had a negative impact on my parents as well.

You see, even when things are going really well, parents will still be worrying about how you're getting along. Anyway, it was decided then and there at the end of my last crisis that I would let my dad know at least once a week how I was doing with work. But at the time, I was wrong to perceive that he was only worried about how much money I was making.

Like my mom, he was worried about my well-being as well. Trust me on this, just as I trust my parents by holding myself accountable to them.

The SMART Goal

Your goals become achievable and are given credence once you've applied a little smartness to the work that needs to go into your goal-setting objectives. And by being smart with your work, you could end up living out the less is more philosophy I introduced to you in Chapter 5.

Even so, writing a smart goal plan for the first time won't be easy. It will take time getting used to the practice, and may even require you to redraw the map you have in front of you every once in a while. But you can pull off this goal-setting objective if you keep the following in mind (*SMART Goals*, n.d.a.):

- Ask yourself what you really need to achieve.

- Ask yourself why you're setting the goals you have in mind.

- Make sure that you can achieve these goals.

- Make sure that these goals are measurable. If they are, then there's a better chance that you'll be able to achieve them.

All About SMART Goal Setting

So, how do you go about creating a SMART goal plan? Well, you could start by following the acronym's objectives to the letter, if you can excuse the pun. Begin by thinking about what the following letters signify (*SMART Goals*, n.d.a.):

- S: Specific (what it is, exactly, that you want to achieve).

- M: Measurable (you can easily tell, at any point, how close you are to your goal, or if you have achieved it).

- A: Achievable (make sure your goal is realistic for the timeframe, your resources, and your abilities).

- R: Relevant (your goal needs to be important to you and what you want).

- T: Time-bound (goals are based on the time you have available, but can also be limited by time, or time-sensitive).

So, if you're bound or restricted by time, you could be asking yourself the following questions to help you overcome these boundaries or limitations (SMART Goals, n.d.a.):

- When could you achieve these goals?

- What could you be doing six months from now?

- What could you be doing six weeks from now?

- What could you be doing today?

Finally, the key takeaways you'll be enjoying by making use of the SMART goals objectives is that your goals will be clear, achievable, and meaningful. That said, you'll be motivated and focused to achieve your goals (*SMART Goals*, n.d.a.).

When SMART Goals Won't Help

If, however, your goal is something that can't be measured, like finding a partner, getting married, and starting a family, then SMART goal setting may not help. In that case, it can help to have a vision board. You might have already heard of these since they have grown in popularity thanks to movies like *The Secret.*

The premise is simple. Get an image of what brings to mind what you want, like pictures of babies or wedding rings, or images of what you want your life to look like in a few years (house, car make and model, career, etc.). Put the images on a board and place the board somewhere you look every day, like your bedroom wall or refrigerator.

Not only does this help remind you of what you are working towards, but it also helps your mind absorb what you want on a subconscious level, making you begin to act in ways that can make what you want possible. The key is to keep thinking it is possible and that you want it. If you start looking at it with a negative attitude and emotions, like doubt, then your subconscious mirrors it. Either it will stop working towards that goal, since you believe it's hopeless, or you'll end up like a character from a "be careful what you wish for" cautionary tale.

Again, this is for goals with no specific timeframe, or that can't be measured. Still, it's something nice to look at everyday.

The Week Ahead

Believe me, I'm already planning the next week, come Friday evening. It's not that I'm now so well organized, as much as I wish that were true. It's just that I'm a little excited about what the new week may bring. But it's at this point that I have to acknowledge that a little anxiety about what may lie ahead still creeps in every once in a while. This is what happens when the past week hasn't gone according to plan.

At this stage, you could perhaps relate. You also worry about the consequences of missing a deadline. You worry about the errors you may have committed as a result of rushing to the finish line. And of course, who doesn't worry about not being paid on time? No, seriously, it really is time to stop worrying. Not only is it time to plan ahead, it's time to plan smartly.

Planning Out Your Week

So, let me use my own planning-ahead regime as a demonstration of planning ahead. It's not a fail-safe plan, and is always subject to change.

For instance, I could be sketching out (mind-mapping) what I would like to do, or need to do (usually it's a bit of both) in the next week. But by the end of the day, it's almost certain that I'll be revisiting that sketch, making changes to it, in accordance with how this final day of the week went.

Then again, there's probably going to be another look at the next week's agenda by the end of Saturday or Sunday. If you're working from home and are, by and large, your own boss, you could relate to this. You see how it goes, particularly if you're passionate or serious about what you're doing, whether you want to or have to, you end up putting in a few extra hours here and there. And there's nothing essentially wrong with this amount of dedication, just as long as you've factored in the requisite breaks I mentioned in an earlier chapter.

Finally, my weekly planner is usually influenced by what I really want to accomplish, and on which days I'd like to see that happening.

What Do You Want to Accomplish, and on Which Days?

What I want to accomplish is also influenced by what is known as good timing. So, if, for instance, something significant related to what I do for a living occurred over the weekend, I might want to get an article out by Monday or Tuesday. Leaving this newsworthy event until the end of the week might result in it becoming yesterday's news, which no one wants to read anyway.

Here's a Plan

But by Monday morning, the rest of the week's agenda must have already been set. For instance, I might have an agreed-to number of words for our next book, which I need to fulfill for my publisher by Friday. That said, I'll need to factor in how many words I could write each day, also taking into account reading and research, and even possible interviews with clients.

At the End of the Day

At the end of the day, not the end of the new week, I'll need to take stock of what I achieved during that day. I'll also need to take note of those tasks that weren't completed during that day. Does this mean that I need to reach for the panic button? No, not at all. All it means is that I will be shifting what was left over from Monday towards the top of the list for Tuesday's schedule, all depending on the complexity of the task, and how long I could be expected to take with it.

How to Debrief Yourself at the End of the Day

At the end of the day, you might not feel like doing anything. You might be exhausted, and more than happy to close the book on your day. But if that is how you're feeling, perhaps you've done too much? Or perhaps you've been distracted at least once during your day (it could be your ADHD symptoms kicking in, for instance)?

Even so, and even if your day went really well, all the more reason to debrief yourself before crashing onto the couch and reaching for the TV remote. The plan that you'll use is not bad, and all you need to do is go through the following three steps to tick off how well (or poorly) you did during the day (Kaplan, 2018):

1. Make a note of all your achievements. But make a note of what went wrong as well.
2. Go through your to-do list, ticking off all that you've completed, but also noting those things you didn't get around to.
3. Plan for the next day, but make sure that you've first evaluated your failures, endeavoring not to repeat past mistakes, perhaps by improving on what you did during the past day.

So, How Well Did You Do?

In the past, I had difficulty with assessing how well I did. That's mostly because I regarded myself as an abject failure. As a result, I would sometimes uncharacteristically lapse into overthinking bouts, further pushing myself into a corner which I couldn't always extricate myself from until I ended up with task paralysis.

I've learned not to lapse into negative thinking habits. This goes for you too. So, even if your day didn't go as well as you would have liked, think about what *did* go well for you during the day. I believe you can do this. I believe you can also metamorphose from what is known as a fixed mindset (it can't be done) to a growth mindset (all things are possible).

I'll be the first to admit that I tend to be a little simple minded at times, but I use this to my advantage. I still like to reward myself if I do very well. I'm pretty big on checklists, because seeing all of those check marks is just so satisfying to me. I have a big white board over my desk with all of my tasks for the day written on there, and a little box next to each task that I can mark as I get the task done. It's simple, but it makes me happy and also keeps me focused.

If I can get at least three fourths of my tasks checked off, I get a cookie. A literal cookie. I will walk my accomplished butt into the kitchen at the end of the day, get a plate and place one, JUST ONE, cookie on it, walk back to the dining area, and enjoy.

Some days, I get my simple slice of happiness, some days, I don't. The point is, that rewards are great to help you look forward to accomplishing a short term goal. It's also important not to beat yourself up if you don't make it, but to go in hungrier the next day, both literally and figuratively for me.

Looking Forward to Tomorrow

Particularly if I've had a rough day–and there will still be those, no matter how well you've planned it–I still look forward to the next day. Perhaps it's more a case of: because today was rough, I look forward to tomorrow. I am positive, believing that the worst is behind me, and that there are better things to look forward to during the next day.

With that positive frame of mind, perhaps that's why my evenings end, so peacefully these days compared to how it was in the past, late nights and all.

The Daily Evening Habit

Indeed, tired or not, I can't wait to go to bed. It's empty by the time I get there, but yes, that would be nice too. I'm not tired to the bone, but am ready to sink into a good night's sleep. The final chapter will talk about how you, too, can get a good night's sleep from now on.

In the meantime, I've done my planning for the next day, and am now focused on doing things that relax me. Cooking is one of those need-to-do activities that do it for me, although it has to be said that I still need to learn to resist the temptation to cook on impulse, even if the ingredients are healthy.

Creating a Review of Your Plan for the Next Day

But before you think of relaxing for the night, don't forget you've still got your planning homework to do. You can relax about that task because the more you become accustomed to it, the easier and quicker it will be for you to complete it. Not that I'm, in any way, suggesting that you rush through this essential task.

So, what to do first? For starters, you'll need to check the agenda for the next day. These will, more than likely, include tasks that need to be fulfilled. Of course, you must include time and space for the things you want to do. Finally, while planning ahead, visualize that you're going to have a successful day (Appelo, 2017).

Incorporating What You Believe Could Have Helped the Day Before

One important thing you need to note in your daily/weekly planner is this: Make a note of whatever's working well. It's a reminder of what can be achieved, and it's something you could incorporate into a new, untried task.

This is also important for utilizing an untested strategy that others have tried (and it worked for them). You still need to make the attempt. Going forward, this will surely allow new, more challenging tasks to become less daunting. It's also ideal for when original plans haven't gone according to it. This, of course, also responds to those unexpected curveballs that life throws at you sometimes.

Dealing With the Curveball

But some of you may be asking: What the heck is a curveball? Yes, you have every right to ask if you're not familiar with baseball or softball. You see, in baseball (and softball), the curveball is a pitch variation thrown with a determined grip and hand movement generated by the pitcher. The pitch generation creates forward spin momentum in the ball, and by the time it reaches the batter's plate, it dives. And when it dives, it dives unexpectedly, so much so that the batter never knows what's coming!

So, that's what life does, it throws you unexpected curveballs. But if you've prepared yourself mentally and physically, and practiced like the MLB's top hitters, then you will be able to handle anything that life throws at you. Well, most of the time anyway. That said, you can use this book's final chapter to help prepare yourself.

CHAPTER 9: SELF-CARE AND WELLNESS

Practicing self-care is your responsibility. You can read many books, including this one, and still not take self-care seriously. It is to be expected during the first stages of your ADHD transformation. You're still hesitant, and you still have your doubts. You may not necessarily doubt the good advice that you've been given, but you may still have doubts about whether or not you're up to the task of taking good care of yourself.

Particularly if you're a caring person by nature, you might also endure feelings of guilt during the early trials of your self-care regime. That's because you might not be used to putting yourself first, leaving others to wait patiently in line, if you will. Of course, I can relate to the negativity because it's as I said right at the beginning after you opened your adult-sized ADHD toolbox for the first time: I've been where you might be right now.

So, in this final chapter, I'm going to be providing you with motivational fuel to help you sustain your transformation from being impulsive and out of control to being calmly in control. Finally, you'll want to exercise care while you create your first-ever self-care and wellness regime, because this is going to be the plan that's going to keep you mentally and physically healthy for the rest of your life.

Healthy Habits for the Rest of Your Healthy Life

Healthy habits for the rest of your healthy life are all good and well, particularly if you're one of those who have always allowed your unhealthy impulses to lead you towards unhealthy indulgences that lead you even further away from your daily, healthy priorities.

You might be one of those who need to fix their eating habits. You might be one of those who need to find reasons to place a genuine smile on your face. You might even need a good night's rest. Rest assured that, from now on, healthy habits for the rest of your healthy life are attainable. And rest assured that all healthy habits are subject to change, meaning of course, that you don't need to subject yourself to dogma or routine. Not that it really matters. After all, you discovered in an earlier chapter of this book that routine doesn't need to be boring.

Incorporating Exercise and Healthy Habits Into Daily Life

A weekly exercise routine doesn't need to be boring, either. There's absolutely no need for you to burn yourself out at a sweaty downtown gym, vainly trying to pump weights if it isn't enjoyable for or in line with how you want to feel. If there is too much you dislike,or the dislike is stronger than what you do enjoy or the joy of what you can get out of the routine, then you'll need a different routine. You won't be able to stick to something that you dread for very long.

Healthy habits become a little easier to incorporate into daily life if you're enjoying them. The same goes for physical exercise, which, of course, doesn't need to include routines and exercises that make you miserable. And even if you are currently overweight, undertraining, rather than overtraining, is a surefire way to start firing up your health for the better.

If you're overweight, it's better to undertrain than to overtrain. It's a classic case of exercising the less is more philosophy to great effect. You won't exhaust yourself on 20 minutes of exercise every other day, as you would with an hour or more, and you'll *still* be getting the same effect. Lightweight training is also good for your mental health, and you won't ever feel as though you're being a burden to yourself, as you would trying to punish yourself, or just giving up altogether.

Healthy habits, like taking the stairs instead of the elevator at work, don't always need to be physical. Indeed, it's sometimes more important that they're benefiting your mental well-being. In my case, nothing beats reading a few pages from one of the books on my current reading list, during one of my longer intermittent breaks. And nothing beats taking a walk downtown in the warm autumn sun before Jack Frost arrives in all earnest.

Productive Self-Reflection

Self-reflection only works if you're prepared to make productive use of the time you've given yourself to self-reflect. It also means that, this time around, you won't be so hard on yourself. Self-criticism is all good and well if you're calm enough to look at yourself in the mirror objectively. However, given where we're coming from, self-reflection is, to my mind, a kinder version of objectifying the way we've been behaving.

But what is self-reflection? Self-reflection is the ability to evaluate cognitive, emotional, and behavioral performance. When done right, you're able to objectively think about the event or behavior, recognize your part, and forgive yourself. This, then leads to finding out why the scenario happened and how it can be better handled or avoided next time. It can also lead to being able to find the root cause of certain behaviors, heal old traumas, and pave the way for better behavior in the future. All good to know, but what if you're in no position to self-reflect?

Therapy and Counseling

If life's currently spinning out of control for you right now, I'd seriously suggest you seek out professional help at the earliest opportunity. There's no shame in doing this, and it's the first sign of improvement in your mental well-being because you're prepared to acknowledge that you have a problem, and it needs to be fixed.

I understand that private practice care may be beyond many folks, but not to worry because there's still the public health service alternative. If it's well-nigh impossible to see a public health practitioner in person (yes, I know, the waiting lines are long), there's always online counseling. I know it's not perfect or ideal, but it's better than no therapy at all.

Finding Your Favorite Creative Outlet

One of the best and most effective ways for you to keep yourself mentally well and physically in good shape is to do the things that you enjoy doing above all else. Of course, this doesn't mean that you're going to act on impulse, drop what you're supposed to be doing, and head off to the pub or mall. Go back to the proper scheduling habits suggested to you in the previous chapter, and you'll soon see, with practice, that there'll be a time and place for everything, especially the things you love.

I recommend a creative outlet, as it can have a longer lasting benefit. Not only would you be able to develop new skill sets, but you would be able to have a healthy outlet for a lot of different emotions.

The best part about it is the satisfaction and happiness that comes from the creative process and the end result. The road to mastery is frustrating at times, but also very rewarding. Unlike instant gratification, the sense of satisfaction is deeper, and the happiness derived from it is much longer lasting than something you've been wanting to buy. After all, there is a reason why many people consider getting everything you want instantly a nasty curse.

The Importance of Making Time for Yourself

In my case, daily walks, sometimes twice-a-day walks, have replaced hours not well spent down at the mall. It's healthier, and of course, requires no charge cards or cash. If spending time indoors constitutes a good break for you (you could be a construction engineer, for instance), then you'll need to make sure that that indoor outlet remains healthy.

If you've got family responsibilities, you need to make it known to them that you, too, need some me-time alone or with friends of your own. And as I said at the beginning of this chapter, doing so is not selfish. It's for your own good, and it's in your family's best interests as well.

Sleeping on What Can't Be Done and Doing What Can Be Done

Both my mom and dad used to worry incessantly about my impulsive, restless nature. While they admired me for my perseverance in doing the things I aspired to, they could always sense the frustration in me when I couldn't get my way. And that's something that used to happen a lot to me back then.

But it was my dad who always used to remind me of the serenity prayer that addicts usually recite during their group therapy sessions. The key line of that prayer that struck a chord with me back then was: *God, grant me the serenity to accept the things I cannot change, the courage to change the things I can, and the wisdom to know the difference.* If only I had had the serenity to take that prayer to heart back then. What a difference it could have made to my life.

Think About the Things You Can Do and Write It Down

It's no use ruminating about what could have been. It's no use ruminating about things that aren't getting done, either. Rather, focus on those things that *can* be done. Because of ADHD distractions, you need to remind yourself of this in your journal.

You can also make a list of the things that you can do, and then start brainstorming ideas on how you can get these things done. Finally, I think it would be awesome if you could make a list of all the things you already have in life that you can be grateful for. You'll soon see that life's not nearly half as bad as you make it out to be.

The Thing About Worrying Is That It Won't

Add One Second to Your Life

My dad, a staunch Christian, used to read Jesus's famous sermon on the Mountain from the book of Matthew to us when our attitudes started to go against our family values. In particular, I recall chapter six of the book of Matthew and how it explains how futile worrying actually is.

It's futile to worry about the things we have no control over. Back in the day, my mom would let her anxieties run rampant. We had to unplug everything in the house before the last person left in case something started a fire. She worried I might be on drugs when I was in high school (I was not), so she would look through my things daily. My mom worried that I wouldn't succeed in college, wouldn't find a job relevant to my major, and would be drowning in debt and living in her basement for years, so she pushed me into real estate as soon as I graduated high school to work with one of my brothers. Being the reclusive introvert that I was, it didn't take long for me to run out of money and quit. This made her anxiety skyrocket, which really wasn't a pretty sight. She finally found a worry she couldn't do anything about and ended up with an ulcer.

Apart from feeling helpless about issues over which you have no control, worrying really isn't good for your health. It can lead to stress related diseases, not to mention self-fulfilling prophecies.

One way to help you stop worrying incessantly is to practice meditation, a practice I introduced to you in Chapter 5. Those were basic exercises to help you relax, but the meditation you could do in this case teaches you to accept your circumstances and surroundings. While following through with the basics of meditation, how you're breathing, for instance, you'll literally be repeating the phrase, "I accept... ." Here, you can spend a few moments reflecting on how you'd like to complete that phrase.

Time to Sleep

Like me back then, if you're still having difficulty in trying to get yourself to fall asleep at night, you can even meditate yourself to sleep. And just like your mom and dad used to do when you were a kid, you could tell yourself bedtime stories as well.

As an adult, I still do this, and I would be embarrassed to reveal to you what stories I tell myself because, really, it's a fantasy world for me before I drift off into La-La-Land. But it would be pointless for me to even tell you what stories I'm telling myself because I wouldn't even be able to remember them, even if I tried.

Guiding Yourself to Sleep

To guide yourself at an appropriate hour (reasonably early, I would think), make use of your journal or notebook to remind you of the key criteria. The two key areas I'd like you to focus on before we prepare to end this chapter are guided sleep meditation, and the creation of a bedtime routine that fits you like a nightcap.

The Guided Sleep Meditation

It goes without saying that you'll be doing this meditation lying down comfortably in bed. And as with the breathing meditation introduced to you earlier, you'll be focusing on your breath. You'll also do a body scan. This entails sensing how your entire body is feeling in the moment, starting from your toes, and working your way up to your crown (*4 Benefits of Sleep Meditation and How To Do It*, 2023).

That said, you'll be focusing on the present moment. And making it easier for you to focus on that moment, you can try visualizing yourself being in a happy place. Because you dearly want to fall asleep like a well-fed baby, I can't imagine that place not being peaceful (*4 Benefits of Sleep Meditation and How To Do It*, 2023).

Finally, you've opened yourself up to letting go of any anxious expectations you might have had about the night ahead, or the next day. You can do this by repeating your very own mantra. If you can't think of anything right now, try repeating "all will be well tomorrow" after each exhalation (*4 Benefits of Sleep Meditation and How To Do It*, 2023).

If you are interested in guided meditations, there are a variety of apps that can help you get started on the right foot. Some come with membership fees, some are free. My favorite thus far is an app called "Let's Meditate," which has a good variety of guided meditations and is free.

Creating a Bedtime Routine That Works

You're welcome to create any routine that works for you. But when you do that, make sure that there's no noise, that the lighting is as dark as you are comfortable with, and that the temperature is cool enough to help you sleep without freezing.

For me, I like to brush my teeth and then take a hot shower. This is the start of the routine I have conditioned myself with. While I'm still comfortably warm, I will turn off the lights, crawl into bed, set my alarm, and begin my sleep meditation. It's to the point now, that I doze off before I'm even halfway through the body scan.

Bedtime Stories

Sometimes, when talking myself to sleep, I sometimes ask, "Why can't I just stop this childish game of fantasy world storytelling?" But then again, as I said to you in the previous chapter, if the system's working, why change it, right? It might seem ridiculous to other folks, but hear them grumble the next morning after you chirpily ask them how they slept last night.

No, you wouldn't do it, that would be cruel. Nevertheless, whichever story you choose to tell yourself at night, is entirely up to you. And if talking yourself is not going to do it for you, you could try reading a few pages from a book on your nightstand, just as long as it's not Dean Koontz or Steven King. It's also prudent to read a physical book instead of a digital copy since the blue light from the screen can keep you up later. Since we've mentioned it so many times earlier, why not pick up a copy of James Joyce's *Ulysses*?

Time to Reflect

I'm almost certain that the mind-bending stream-of-consciousness of *Ulysses* will exhaust you. What shouldn't exhaust you, however, is your daily exercise, not even your evening meals. You may recall that Thanksgiving feeling at the end of a heavy three-course meal. You're feeling bloated, and all you want to do is go take a nap. It's not healthy, and if you're at risk, it's not good for your heart either.

Another thing that shouldn't exhaust you is worrying and overthinking while you're trying to sleep. One of the benefits of meditation is that it can help with rumination. Just like when you meditate, acknowledge the thought, thank your mind for it, and let it pass. Is the thought going to determine the difference of whether you will live or die? Chances are, the answer is a no.

If it is still impossible to even focus on a guided meditation or bedtime story, then it might help to briefly turn on the light and write down what is on your mind. That way, your mind can rest at ease a little bit better knowing that you've acknowledged the thought and have it on a list for the morning. With no reason to keep it in mind since it is written down, your mind will forget it like all the memorized phone numbers those of us born before the year 2000 have forgotten.

So, now that this final chapter is completed, it's time to reflect on what you've learned and experienced from your reading of *An Adult ADHD Toolkit*.

CONCLUSION

By now, you must surely be patting yourself on the back. And if I were in your company right now, I'm confident in the knowledge that I'll be one of the beneficiaries of a healthy smile from you. It's not that we'll be happy to see each other (we will be, of course, we will!), it's just that you'll be happy with the progress you've made so far.

Indeed, if you've read every single page of *An Adult ADHD Toolkit*, you *have* made progress in your life. I'm quite certain that, by now, you will have tested a handful of the tips and suggestions that have been put forward throughout this book. You'll have done the testing after discovering that it's not as laborious as it looked on paper. And I'm confident that you will have experienced a positive change in how you perceive yourself, how you're behaving, and how you're managing whatever circumstances you're faced with on a daily basis.

Reflecting on Progress Made

The conclusion to this book is yours to write, so at this stage, I'm not going to reflect too much on what we've covered in this book. But what I would like you to do is tell us what you think of the work we've done for you. You can use the space provided to leave us a short note.

But if you're stuck for words, that's okay. Perhaps you need a little more time and practice with your journal writing and note-taking. Now, ordinarily, I would advise to not worry about grammar mistakes, sentence constructions, and typos. After all, nobody but yourself is going to be peering into your book of life.

But after careful reflection, I would like you to take pride in the way you write, and the way you express yourself in writing. Not only will you understand everything that you've written, and not only will everything be legible to you, you'll feel better about yourself, and what you've produced. You don't need to turn your journal into a literary work of art overnight, but could set aside time during a quieter part of the week to practice, and polish your craft. Heck, you could treat this as a new hobby, amongst other ideas you might have in your back pocket right now.

In the meantime, let me continue motivating you to make progress in your life, right to the very end of this book's final page. Let me continue providing you with reassurance that it's going to be okay living with ADHD. You might not be able to get rid of the symptoms altogether, but at least you now know that you'll be able to manage them. Like me going for a sunny walk instead of down to the mall, you'll also have found something healthy and delightful to replace the things that have usually tempted your impulses, right up to the moment you started reading this book.

Continuing the Journey Towards a Happier, More Focused Life

This book is yours to keep. It's yours to re-use at will. So, whenever you feel as though you're slipping up in areas of your life, you can use the suggestions provided to help you back onto the path you chose to take when you purchased this book. That choice is to learn how to overcome your ADHD symptoms, deal with it, and manage it, and continue with your journey towards a happier, more focused life.

Don't Stop Thinking About Tomorrow

Because Yesterday's Gone

At one point, I couldn't help myself during the writing of the draft to the book's conclusion. I was thinking about what I would be doing tomorrow. And I was thinking about what I would be doing once this book was put to rest. What project would I be working on next? Would I be giving self-help therapy a short rest in order to satisfy one of my other literary passions?

One thing I can tell you is that I won't be returning to James Joyce's *Ulysses* any day soon. Just you try reading it someday, and you'll see what I mean, although I have to say that you could use this modern literary classic of over 1000 pages as a practical exercise to help you train yourself to focus better. You wouldn't need to read the entire book, and could just focus on a few pages at a time, and see if you can manage the literary genius's syntax, sentence constructions, and language and grammatical register.

See it as a game of chess, or even a game of patience, if you can excuse the pun. Of course, you have to love reading as much as I do, to brace yourself for the challenge. In the meantime, all I can say is that I won't be attempting to read this giant tome backwards. I don't need to, my ADHD symptoms are well under control by now.

While I was writing the final sentences of this draft, I couldn't help thinking about the old Fleetwood Mac song, *Don't Stop Thinking About Tomorrow*. I've taken liberties with the song's title, if that's okay with Stevie Nicks and Lindsey Buckingham, because I wanted to highlight the importance of *not* thinking too deeply about what tomorrow could bring, even though you've planned for it well enough. I also want to highlight the importance of not looking too much at your past for answers on why you still behave the way you do today.

That said, it's still okay to use your past for self-reflection purposes, and to help you not only learn from them, but to triumph over the mistakes you may have made in the past. Most importantly, I want to emphasize the importance of learning to live and be in the present moment. You can use meditation exercises to help you get to that point, and when you do, not only will you be able to focus better on what's directly in front of you, but you'll be at peace with your surroundings.

Even on trying days, you'll be close to having what is known as the patience of Job. Job was a wealthy guy from Biblical times who could do no wrong. He wasn't dealing with ADHD or any other mental disorders. He had everything going for him, until one day, quite literally overnight, he lost everything, all that he had spent years working towards. Finally, the story of Job is really about one man's struggle to overcome all obstacles, before squashing them, and celebrating all that life has got to offer.

I dare say that your life hasn't even been half as bad as his was, but my moral of this story is that if he can do it, then so can you. And if I can overcome and master ADHD in a matter of months (for others, it might take longer), then so can you.

So then, what are you waiting for? Saddle up, and get on with the rest of your life. Oh, and one more thing. Pay attention. Your happiness depends on it.

REFERENCES

Appelo, J. (2017, August 2). *Daily Planning — Prepare for the Next Day*. https://medium.com/@jurgenappelo/daily-planning-prepare-for-the-next-day-8524f90d69c1

Attention-Deficit/Hyperactivity Disorder (ADHD). (n.d.a.). Cleveland Clinic. https://my.clevelandclinic.org/health/diseases/4784-attention-deficithyperactivity-disorder-adhd#:~:text=Scientists%20have%20discovered%20there%20are,own%20emotions%2C%20thoughts%20and%20actions.

Chia, S. (2023, April 7). *15 ways to improve your focus and concentration*. https://www.betterup.com/blog/15-ways-to-improve-your-focus-and-concentration-skills

Cope, S. (2021, April 1). *18 Effective Time Management Strategies and Techniques*. https://www.upwork.com/resources/time-management-strategies

Ekman, P. (1994). *The Nature of Emotion: Fundamental Questions (Series in Affective Science)*. Oxford University Press.

Farag, A. (2023, June 18). *The Minimalist Movement: Why Less is the New More*. https://www.linkedin.com/pulse/minimalist-movement-why-less-new-more-amr-farag/

5 Conflict Resolution Strategies We All Use. (2016, June 5) The Participation Company. https://theparticipationcompany.com/2016/06/5-conflict-resolution-strategies/#:~:text=Kenneth%20Thomas%20and%20Ralph%20Kilmann,to%20be%20in%20a%20conflict.

Flippin, R. (2023, August 25). *Hyperfocus: The ADHD Phenomenon of Intense Fixation.* https://www.additudemag.com/understanding-adhd-hyperfocus/

4 Benefits of Sleep Meditation and How To Do It. (2023, May 12). Cleveland Clinic. https://health.clevelandclinic.org/sleep-meditation/

Gattig, N. (2023, April 27). *18 effective strategies to improve your communication skills.* https://www.betterup.com/blog/effective-strategies-to-improve-your-communication-skills

Hoff, B. (1982) *The Tao of Pooh.* Penguin Books.

Hoff, B. (1992) *The Te of Piglet.* Penguin Books.

Kaplan, K. (2018, October 16). *How to Productively End Your Work Day With a Daily Debrief.* https://www.kristinkaplan.com/blog/HowtoProductivelyEndYourWorkDay

Kouly, M. (2023, July 28). *Harness Your Strengths, Overcome Your Weaknesses.* https://www.linkedin.com/pulse/harness-your-strengths-overcome-weaknesses-michael-kouly-/

Lema, C. (n.d.a.). *Managing The Chaos.* https://www.leaders.blog/managing-organized-chaos/

Living with Attention deficit hyperactivity disorder (ADHD). (n.d.a.). National Health Service. https://www.nhs.uk/conditions/attention-deficit-hyperactivity-disorder-adhd/living-with/

McRae, L. (2019, September 25). *How to Start a New Routine and Stick To It.* https://www.northshore.org/healthy-you/how-to-start-a-new-routine-and-stick-to-it/

Mandriota, M. (2022, April 12). *Can ADHD Affect Your Social Skills?* https://psychcentral.com/adhd/adhd-social-skills

Norepinephrine (Noradrenaline). (2022, March 27). Cleveland Clinic. https://my.clevelandclinic.org/health/

articles/22610-norepinephrine-noradrenaline#:~:text=Norepinephrine%2C%20also%20known%20as%20noradrenaline,short%2Dterm%20serious%20health%20situations.

Real-World Strategies: "How I Stop Being So Impulsive". (2022, March 31). Additude Mag. https://www.additudemag.com/how-do-i-stop-being-impulsive-adhd/

Riopel, L. (2019, November 28). *28 Best Meditation Techniques for Beginners to Learn.* https://positivepsychology.com/meditation-techniques-beginners/

Rivero, L. (2018, January 27). *How ADHD Adults Cope Before Treatment.* https://www.psychologytoday.com/au/blog/creative-synthesis/201801/how-adhd-adults-cope-before-treatment#:~:text=Littman%2C%20PhD%2C%20gives%20the%20example,by%20social%20stimuli%2C%20or%20even

Rysdyk, E. (n.d.a.) *The Power of Creative Energy.* https://www.innertraditions.com/blog/the-power-of-creative-energy

Signs you might be experiencing a burnout and how to regain balance in your life. (2021, November 22). Darling Downs Health. https://www.darlingdowns.health.qld.gov.au/about-us/our-stories/feature-articles/signs-you-might-be-experiencing-a-burnout-and-how-to-regain-balance-in-your-life

Silver, L. (2022, July 13). *ADHD Neuroscience 101.* https://www.additudemag.com/adhd-neuroscience-101/#:~:text=ADHD%20was%20the%20first%20disorder,is%20synthesized%20within%20the%20brain.

Springett, D. (2023, February 14). *Triage Your To-Do List.* https://www.linkedin.com/pulse/triage-your-to-do-list-dawn-springett/

SMART Goals. (n.d.a.). Mind Tools. https://docs.google.com/document/d/1UR3Vwl61eZqHlQdsHwhpvMQqKZw3tysEJuswu09xFvY/edit

Stream of Consciousness. (n.d.a.). Litcharts. https://www.litcharts.com/literary-devices-and-terms/stream-of-consciousness#:~:text=Stream%20of%20consciousness%20writing%20allows,and%20move%20through%20the%20mind.

The Neuroscience of Behavior Change. (2017, August 8). Health Transformer. https://healthtransformer.co/the-neuroscience-of-behavior-change-bcb567fa83c1

Tips for Managing Conflict. (n.d.a.). Clarke University. https://www.clarke.edu/campus-life/health-wellness/counseling/articles-advice/tips-for-managing-conflict/

Walsh, A. (2022, April 19). *5 Ways to Make Sure You Achieve Your Goals This Year*. https://hbr.org/2022/04/4-ways-to-make-sure-you-achieve-your-goals-this-year

Watson, S. (2022, August 25). *ADHD in the Workplace*. https://www.webmd.com/add-adhd/adhd-in-the-workplace

What Can Trigger ADHD in Adults?. (2023, March 6). The ADHD Centre. https://www.adhdcentre.co.uk/what-can-trigger-adhd-in-adults

What is ADHD? (n.d.a.) Psychiatry. https://www.psychiatry.org/patients-families/adhd/what-is-adhd

Wilkins, F. (2023, May 2). *How Is the ADHD Brain Different?* https://childmind.org/article/how-is-the-adhd-brain-different/#differences-in-neurochemistry

Wisner, W. (2023, July 17). *How a Brain Dump Can Help You Relieve Stress*. https://www.verywellmind.com/what-is-a-brain-dump-7111793

NOTES

Notes

Notes

Notes

Notes

Notes